the EVERYONE series

Badminton everyone

C. Charlie Song
Texas Tech University

Ming Li
Georgia Southern University

Hunter Textbooks Inc.

Acknowledgments

We would like to thank the many individuals who helped to complete this book. Mr. Yongbo Li, the Head Coach of the Chinese National Badminton Team (also the world champion in men's doubles during the 1980s), served us as our technical advisor and supported us tremendously by letting the world's best players on his team demonstrate the techniques in this book. In the meantime, he has left us with a great friendship to keep in the future.

Thanks also to coaches, Mr. Bingyi Tian (former world champion in men's doubles paired with Mr. Yongbo Li), Ms. Lingwei Li (the world's No. 1 player in ladies singles during the 1980s), and Mr. Mao Li (three time Thomas Cup winner in men's singles) for their generous cooperation and support. Other coaches whom we could not name here also deserve our sincere appreciation.

Thanks to Yaru Liu and Pidi Zhang, our friends and photographers.

We would like to thank the players who served as models for the photos. Their patience in demonstrating their skills as well as their wonderful personalities made the photo shoot a pleasant experience. These players and their IBF ranking at the time the photos were taken are listed below:

Jiong Dong	First, men's singles
Zhaoying Ye	First, women's singles
Fei Ge	First, ladies' doubles and mixed doubles
Jun Gu	First, ladies' doubles
Wei Zhang	Ninth, men's doubles

Finally, a special thanks to Charlie's wife, Ladonice Song, who helped us edit the entire book.

Charlie Song
Ming Li

Printed in the United States of America.

ISBN 0-88725-283-4

Inquiries should be addressed to:

HTI Hunter Textbooks Inc.

701 Shallowford St.
Winston-Salem, NC 27101

Table of Contents

Chapter 1

Badminton: Then and Now

Badminton is a fascinating sport enjoyed by millions of people of all ages. It is played by two to four players on a court divided by a net. Badminton can be played either indoors or outdoors, although all formal competitions are held indoors. The players use rackets to propel a shuttlecock across the net. This is called rallying or volleying. The shuttlecock must not touch the ground during a rally. The shuttlecock's conical design and feather construction make it capable of a wide variety of speeds. The flight characteristics of the shuttlecock and the pace created by constant volleying make badminton one of the most exciting sports to play and watch.

In most formal competitions, five events are scheduled: men's singles, men's doubles, women's singles, women's doubles and mixed doubles. The best two of three games decides the match, and there is no time limit for a match. All games are determined in fifteen points except for women's singles which is eleven points.

Badminton Then: Origins and Development

The history of badminton dates back to Ancient Greece and the early Far-Eastern civilization. A game similar to badminton was depicted on pottery around 3,000 years ago in China. This purely recreational game was sometimes played using the player's feet instead of rackets. A game called "Poona" played in India at least 2,000 years ago was also similar to badminton, as well as "battledore" or "shuttlecock" which was played in England, Sweden and Denmark during ancient times.

A competitive version of badminton was developed in India and England in the mid- and late-nineteenth century. Badminton, as we know it today, adopted its name from Badminton House in Gloucestershire, England—home of the Duke of Beaufort. Since then the game of badminton has gained tremendous popularity in many countries around the world. It is a major sport in many European and Southeastern Asian countries.

The earliest national organization for badminton, the Badminton Association of England, was established in 1893. The first All-England Championship was held in 1897. It is the oldest international tournament for badminton and attracts many of the world's top players.

The Badminton Club of New York was formed in the winter of 1878-1879 by two British players, Bayard Clark and E. Langdon (Landon) Wilkes. In 1936, The American Badminton Association was organized and in 1937 held the first national championship. The championships were played on 21 courts in Chicago. The American Badminton Association was called the United States Badminton Association (USBA) until 1996. Now, it is known as USA Badminton (USAB).

The International Badminton Federation (IBF) was founded in 1934 with nine members—Canada, Denmark, England, France, Ireland, Netherlands, New Zealand, Scotland and Wales. The United States joined four years later. Its membership has grown steadily over the years with a surge in new members after badminton's Olympic debut at Barcelona in 1992. Currently there are 138 IBF member associations around the world.

In 1948, the IBF held its first major tournament, Thomas Cup, the men's team world championship. The women's team world championship, Uber Cup, was first held in 1957.

Badminton Now: An Increasingly Popular Sport

Since the first Thomas Cup and Uber Cup, the number of IBF's major world events has increased to seven; they are: the World Championships, the Sudirman Cup (mixed team), the World Juniors, the World Grand Prix Finals and the World Cup. The World Cup series organized by the International Management Group (IMG) ended in 1997. The IBF, however, is considering organizing a series of tournaments featuring the world's top players to replace the World Cup.

According to IBF sources, a watershed in badminton's growth was the $20 million contract in 1994 for sponsorship of the World Grand Prix Finals. For the 1996 Thomas Cup and Uber Cup in Hong Kong, the commercial and television rights contracts were worth millions of dollars. Badminton is a very spectacular and exciting sport among the events in Olympic Games competitions. During the 1996 Atlanta

Badminton medal presentation at the 1996 Summer Olympics.

Olympic Games, for example, badminton was a "sell-out" event. Former president Jimmy Carter, First Daughter Chelsea Clinton, Princess Anne and Paul Newman were among the celebrities in the audience at the badminton competitions. It was estimated that more than 1.1 billion people around the world watched the badminton competitions on television during the 1996 Olympic Games.

Badminton has certainly captured many hearts in Asia and Europe and continues to gain in popularity in the United States. The only time the Uber Cup was won outside Asia was in 1957, 1960, and 1963 by the Team USA. American Judy Hashman also set a record number of seventeen All-England titles.

The two most successful nations in badminton are China and Indonesia; together they have won about 70% of all IBF events. Since the 1948 Thomas Cup, the men's world's team championship has been won by three countries—China, Indonesia, and Malaysia. Indonesia has won 11 of the last 20 Thomas Cups. China, Indonesia, and Japan have dominated Uber Cup, the women's world team championship. Chinese women currently seat five spots among the world's top seven singles players and are ranked first and second for doubles according to the IBF ranking.

Denmark has become a strong challenger to the Asian dominance in the world of badminton. Denmark has reached either the finals or semifinals in the most recent Thomas Cups. Danish players have demonstrated their strength in singles competitions, particularly men's singles. Poul-Erik Hoyer-Larsen won the Men's Singles Gold Medal for Denmark in the 1996 Olympic Games. According to the IBF ranking in August 1998, Danish players were ranked at the top for men's singles and second for ladies' singles.

Chapter 2

Benefits of Playing Badminton

Badminton is a lifetime sport that can be played by men, women and children of all ages with a minimum of expense and effort. As leisure time increases, badminton plays a more important role in the fitness and recreational programs in American society. Because of the construction of the shuttlecock, badminton can be played with various levels of physical effort depending on the players' conditions.

Badminton is a very entertaining sport as well as the fastest racket sport. The speed of a shuttlecock can reach up to 200 miles per hour (m.p.h.). The conical structure of the shuttlecock adds to the sport's enormous unpredictability, forcing competitive players to develop speed, agility, flexibility and physical endurance. Playing badminton is also mentally stimulating. Psychological toughness is a *must* for good players. Mental agility, especially related to game strategy, may earn a player as many points as physical skills.

Competitive badminton players must develop speed, agility and physical endurance.

Aerobic benefits from playing singles between skilled badminton opponents are equal or greater than that of tennis for a similar amount of time. A player volleys with his or her opponent on an area of 22 feet by 17 feet. Because badminton features a fast paced and unpredictable shuttlecock, players build a strong cardiovascular and respiratory capacity. Badminton doubles can be even more challenging than singles play. The doubles game leaves less reaction time for players and provides a great opportunity for developing cooperation between partners. The differences between singles and doubles make badminton even more enjoyable to play or watch.

Easy to learn basic techniques make badminton a pleasurable sport for any age or fitness level. Developing skills and understanding playing strategies allow more experienced players continued enjoyment. Appreciation of the game can be enhanced by playing often and watching other players' matches, particularly skilled players' competitions.

Chapter 3

The Court and Equipment

The Court

Badminton is played in a rectangular court with measurements of 17 feet by 44 feet for singles play and 20 feet by 44 feet for doubles play. (See Figure 3.1.) The lines drawn on the court are 1 ½ inches (40 mm) wide. Because the lines must be easily distinguishable, they are usually colored white or yellow.

Figure 3.1: The badminton court

The net divides the court into two equal sections. The net is made of fine cord of a dark color and is 2'6" (760 mm) high. The top of the net is edged with a 3" (75 mm) white tape doubled over a cord or cable which runs the length of the net. The top of the net to the surface of the court is 5' (1.524 m) at the center of the court and 5'1" (1.55 m) over the sidelines for doubles. There should be no gaps between the ends of the net and the post.

Figure 3.2 illustrates the marking of areas on the court. The doubles service end lines are 2'6" (780 mm) from the back boundary lines toward the net. The doubles sidelines are marked 1'6" (468 mm) outside from the singles sidelines.

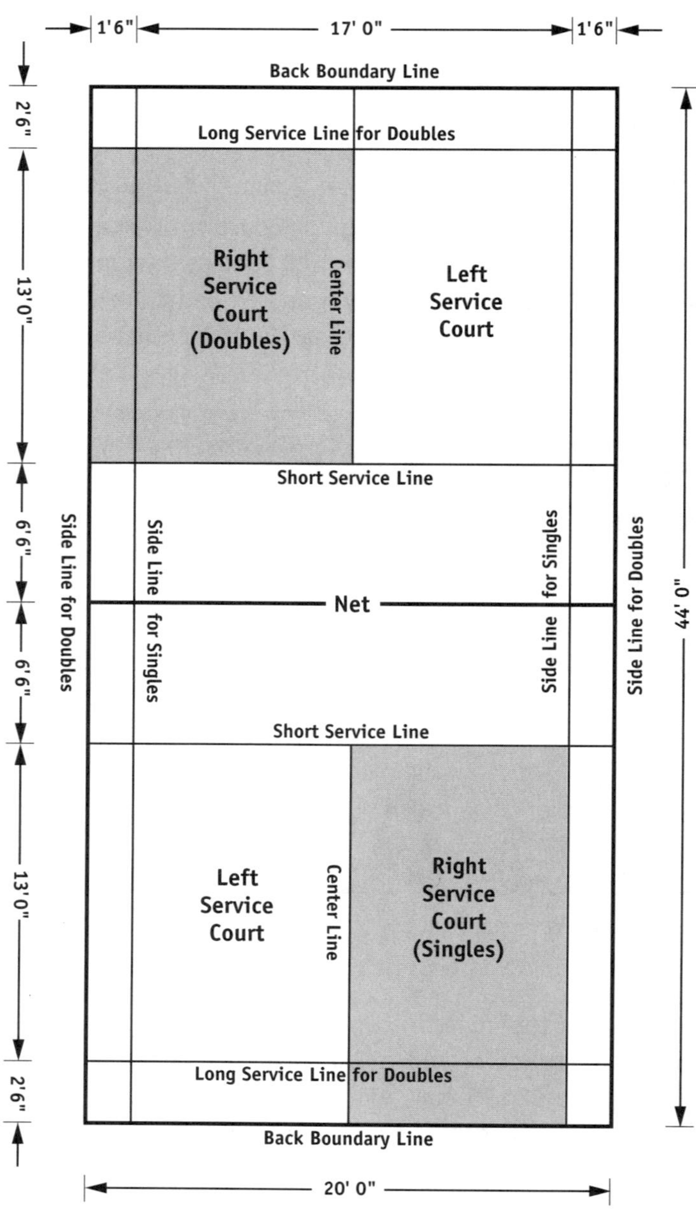

Figure 3.2: Markings of the badminton court

To show the zone, in which a shuttlecock hit at the correct speed lands when tested, an additional four marks of 1 ½" by 1 ½" (40 mm by 40 mm) may be made inside each sideline for singles of the right service court. The marks are 1'9" (530 mm) and 3'1" (950 mm) from the back boundary line. (See Figure 3.3.)

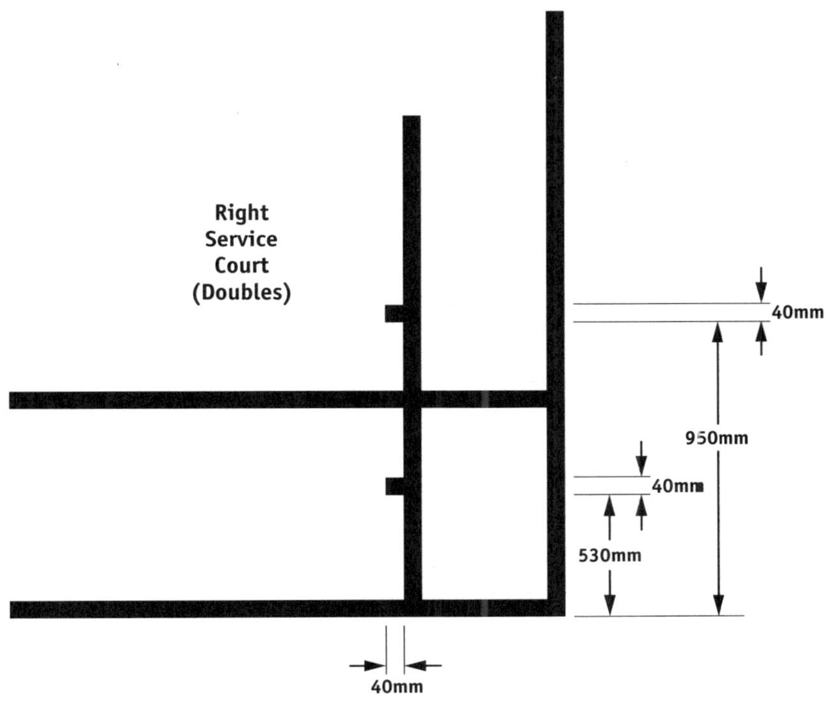

Figure 3.3: Zone for testing shuttlecock speed

When the game is played indoors, the ceiling should not be less than 30 feet over the full court area. This space should be entirely free from girders and other obstructions. There should be at least 4 feet of clear floor space surrounding each court and between any two courts.

Equipment

Rackets

Figure 3.4: The racket

The racket is constructed of three sections: the head, the shaft and the grip. (See Figure 3.4.) For a long time rackets were made entirely of wood. Shafts made of steel or fiberglass were introduced in the 1950s. Virtually all quality rackets are now constructed of various blends of steel, aluminum, boron, carbon and graphite. Most of the world's top players use carbon graphite shaft rackets. These rackets are very light (around 3.5 ounces) and so strong that they can be strung much tighter than earlier rackets. A racket's overall dimensions cannot exceed 2' 2 $\frac{3}{4}$" (680 mm) by 9" (230 mm) and the length of the head should not exceed 11 $\frac{3}{8}$" (290 mm).

Rackets are strung with animal gut or synthetic string. A racket should be strung with 15 to 20 pounds of tension. A racket cover protects the strings when the racket is not in use. Handle grips are normally made of leather. Replacement grips made of leather, gauze or towel are commonly used.

Shuttlecocks

Figure 3.5: The shuttlecock

The shuttlecock may also be called by other names, such as shuttle, birdie and bird. (See Figure 3.5.) The feathered shuttlecock is used in all major competitions. The feathered shuttle weighs from 4.74 to 5.50 grams and is made of 16 goose feathers inserted into a leather-covered cord base. The heavier shuttle flies faster in normal circumstances.

There are also a number of different brands of synthetic shuttlecocks available, particularly for recreational use and school play. These synthetic shuttles may have slightly different flight characteristics from the feathered ones. According to the IBF, the synthetic shuttle is acceptable for competition if it differs less than 10% in its gravity and flying characteristics from the feathered shuttle.

Feathered shuttles cost more than synthetic shuttles, but do not last as long. Shuttles, especially the feathered shuttles, last much longer if they are humidified. Humidified shuttles become heavier, and therefore, fly faster.

Each time a game is played during a competition or tournament, the shuttle should function at the same speed regardless of atmospheric conditions. The testing of a shuttle's speed takes place at the beginning of a match. To perform the test, players hit the shuttle with a full underhand stroke at an upward angle from a spot close to one back boundary line in a direction parallel to the sidelines. The shuttle should land not less than 1'9" (530 mm) and not more than 3'3" (990 mm) short of the other back boundary line. (See Figure 3.3 for details about the test zone.)

Other Accessories

The clothing for badminton play is rather casual. The usual dress for both men and women is shirt and shorts. Optional wristbands aid in absorption of perspiration around the hands. The footwear worn on a badminton court should be an athletic shoe that has excellent traction and supports shifting body weight and abrupt lateral movement on the court. There are some specific shoes made for serious badminton players. Tennis shoes are also acceptable.

Other accessories include specially designed bags for badminton which provide a racket compartment, shoe pocket, clothing section, as well as a string pocket. A racket glove or head cover is commonly used to protect the strings. (See Figure 3.6)

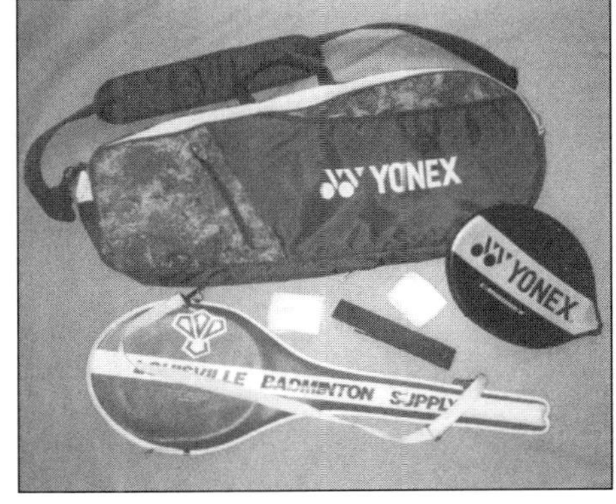

Figure 3.6: Other accessories

Chapter 4

Rules of Play

The International Badminton Federation (IBF) publishes the Statutes containing the Laws of Badminton as well as the interpretations and revisions of the Laws. This book can be obtained from the IBF. (Information about the IBF can be found in Resources.) The Laws of Badminton are reprinted in their full content in the Appendix of this book. The Laws change from time to time and a current official Statutes should be consulted for any tournament play.

Simplified Laws of Badminton

Players

Players are those persons taking part in the game. There is one player on a side in singles play and two players on a side in doubles play.

Toss

Before a game begins, the players toss a coin or spin a racket. The winner of the toss or spin has an option of serving first, receiving first, or choosing the end of the court. The player losing the toss or spin has a choice of the remaining options.

Serving

Play begins by a serve. A player can score only when he or she is serving. The server and receiver stand in the service courts diagonally opposite each other. The serve at the start of a game is always from the service court on the right. The service court areas are different for singles and doubles. After serving, a player may move anywhere on his or her side of the net. As stated in the Laws of Badminton, the serve must be underhanded, and the receiver must stand still until the service is completed. A shuttle on the line is "in."

Serving Rotation

In singles, the players serve from and receive in the right service court when the server's score is an even number. (See Figure 4.1.1.) The players serve from and receive in the left service court when the server's score is an odd number. (See Figure 4.1.2.)

Figure 4.1.1: Serving at an even number of points (singles)

Figure 4.1.2: Serving at an odd number of points (singles)

In doubles, the side serving first in a game has only one turn at serve and the service is in the right service court. The server alternates service courts (switching with his or her partner) as long as rallies are won, but the receiver does not switch positions with his or her partner. (See Figures 4.2.1 and 4.2.2.)

Figure 4.2.1: First serve at an even number of points (doubles)

4.2.2: First serve at an odd number of points (doubles)

After the first serving side loses a rally at the very beginning of the game, service passes to the opposing side. From this point on, both players on a side have a turn to serve before the service passes to the opposing side. The player who is in the right service court, due to the team's score at the time, strikes the service. He or she may continue the serve until a rally is lost, then the "second server" serves without changing court position with his or her partner. The second server continues the service and alternates courts after each serve until a rally is lost. Then the serve goes to the opposing side. (See Figures 4.3.1 and 4.3.2).

Figures 4.3.1 and 4.3.2: The second server continues the service

In doubles, when the serving team's score is an even number, the server must be standing in the service court (either right or left) in which he or she started the game. (See Figure 4.4.1.)

When the score is an odd number, however, the server should be in the opposite service court (right or left). (See Figure 4.4.2.)

Figures 4.4.1 and 4.4.2: When the score is an even number, the server remains standing in the same service court in which she started.

The receiving team's players stand in positions wherever their score defines them to be. The receiving players do not alternate positions even when the server does. (See Figures 4.5.1 and 4.5.2.) After the serve is delivered, players on both teams may take any position on the court.

Figures 4.5.1 and 4.5.2: The receiving players do not alternate positions

Scoring

Each game starts at 0:0 (called "love-all"). The player wins a rally if he or she hits the shuttle over the net and onto the floor of the opponent's side of the court. Each time a player wins a rally while serving, he or she scores one point, alternates service courts and serves again. If the receiving side wins the rally, the score remains unchanged and the service passes to the opponent in singles or to the next player in rotation in doubles.

Men's singles and doubles games consist of 15 points; ladies' singles, 11 points. A "set" can be called if the score is tied at 14:14 (called "14-all") in a 15 point game or at "10-all" in an 11 point game; the player who reached 14 (10) first has the privilege to "set" the game to 3 for a total of 17 (13) points, or to continue the game to 15 (11) points. The following chart indicates the rules of "setting."

Points in Game	Score Tied at	Game May Be Set To
11	10 all	3 points
15	14 all	3 points

A match is comprised of the best of three games. The players change sides of the court at the end of each game and when the leading score reaches 8 (or 6 for ladies' singles) in the third game. A five-minute interval is allowed prior to any third game.

Faults

When a violation of the Laws (a fault) occurs on the serving side, no point is scored and the serve passes to the next appropriate server. If a fault occurs on the receiving side, the serving side scores a point. The following faults are common in a badminton game.

Faults during Serving and Receiving

Regardless of executing a forehand or backhand serve, the head of the racket must be below the waist level of the server and the grip must be above the head of the racket on contact. (See Figure 4.6 for the front view and Figure 4.7 for the side view.) Figure 4.8 illustrates a typical faulty movement for a backhand serve in which the head of the racket is above the server's wrist and higher than the server's waist level.

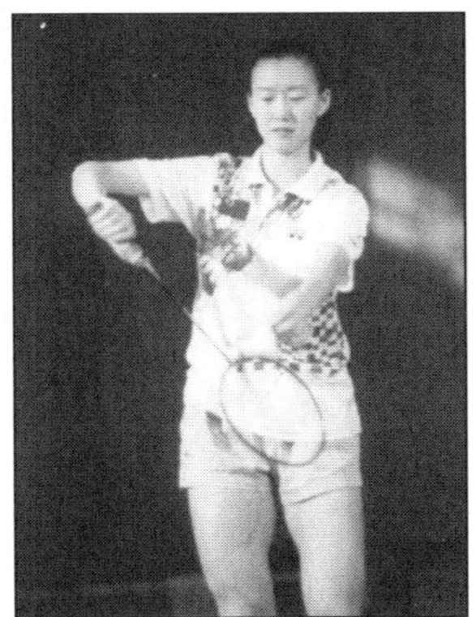

Figure 4.6: Front view of the serve

Figure 4.7: Side view of the serve

Figure 4.8: Faulty backhand serve

The server's feet must be stationary in the correct service position. Part of both of the server's feet must be in contact with the surface of the court from the start of the service until the service is delivered. (See Figure 4.9.)

Figure 4.9: Proper feet position during serve

If any unusual occurrence interferes with the play before the next service is delivered, a "let" (replay of the point) can be invoked. This happens, for example, if a shuttle from a nearby court interferes or if a line judge and the umpire are unable to make a decision on whether a particular shot is in-bounds or out.

Faults during Play

See the Appendix: The Laws of Badminton.

Officiating

In all national and international competitions, the officials needed to conduct a match are an umpire, service judge and ten line judges. In addition, an adequate number of recorders are needed to keep the scores. In local or school competitions, matches are conducted either with or without officials.

The umpire is the chief official of a match. He or she calls the score, rules on receiving faults and enforces the Laws. The service judge rules on service faults. The line judges determine if the shuttle is "in" or "out" when it lands on the court floor. The umpire is the ultimate decision-maker to rule a play. Figure 4.10 shows the position of officials for a match. U refers the umpire, SJ to the service judge, and L to line judges. For more detailed definitions of the officials' duties, see the Appendix: Laws of Badminton.

L = Line judge
SJ = Service judge
U = Umpire

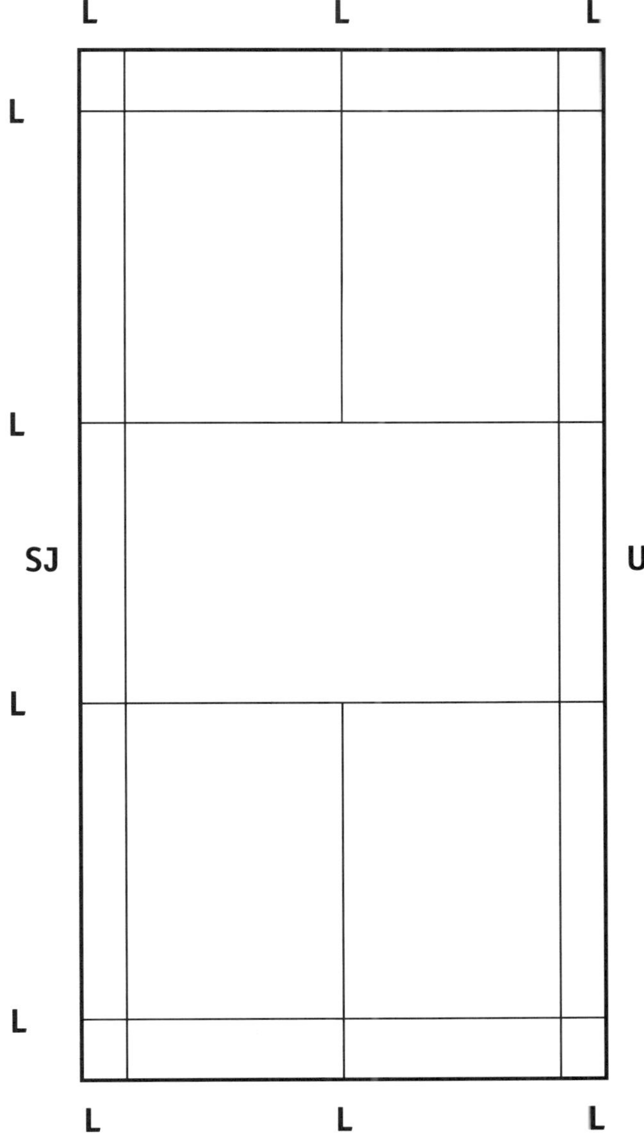

Figure 4.10: Positions of officials during a badminton match

Common Etiquette in Badminton

Badminton, like many other sports, has its own courtesies and etiquette. These are the unwritten rules that are observed on the courts.

- Hit the shuttle directly to your opponent during the warmup.
- Start the warmup with deep overhead clears.
- Agree upon the shuttle selected for use.
- Before serving, call the score at each point and be sure your opponent is ready.
- Call the fault on yourself promptly.
- Let your opponent make line calls on his or her side of the net and don't question your opponent's call.
- Ask your opponent first when you wish to change the shuttle.
- Pick up shuttles on your side of the net and nearest to you. Pass the shuttle to your opponent when he or she is ready. Avoid shoving the shuttle under the net.
- Play at your best game; even if your opponent is not compatible to your skills. It is insulting to your opponent to do otherwise.
- Always shake hands and thank your opponent after the match.
- Finally, either as a recreational participant or a competitive player, it is important to always exhibit good sportsmanship.

Chapter 5

Basic Technical Elements in Badminton

There are four basic technical elements in the completion of each stroke. Once the player determines where the shuttle will drop, the player quickly moves from the ready position to the drop point and executes the return. Then, the player immediately returns to the center of the court to get ready for the next shot. The four technical elements of a badminton stroke are taking a ready stance, making a judgment and taking off, positioning the body and setting up the racket, and hitting the shuttle and returning to the center of the court. These four elements form a cycle. (See Figure 5.1.)

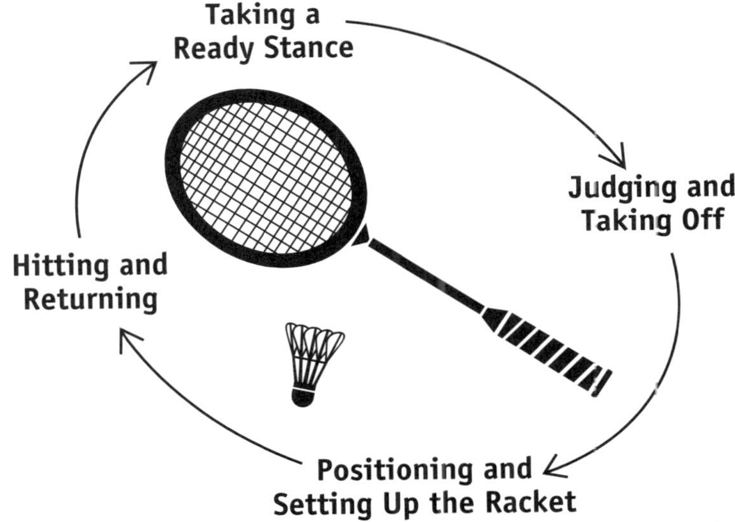

Figure 5.1: Four elements of the badminton stroke

Players on both sides take turns repeating this cycle until the rally is over. All the elements in the cycle are intertwined with each other and the failure to execute any of them may greatly affect the technical quality of each stroke performed.

Taking a Ready Stance

At the beginning of each round of rally, both the server, after delivering the service, and the receiver, who is preparing for the reception, should position themselves where they can move to any spot on their side of the court efficiently. The players should also take a stance that may help them to take off promptly. (See the section on the Ready Position in Singles in Chapter 6 for details.)

Judging and Taking off

The player should anticipate the type of stroke that the opponent will use in making the return. Such anticipation usually comes from determining the opponent's strategic intent, striking patterns, playing technique and the actual return. By doing so, the player can shift his or her center of gravity toward the anticipated shuttle's drop point in advance and possibly move to this point prior to or at the moment when the returning stroke is made. However, according to the Laws of Badminton, it is illegal for the receiver to make any movement before the shuttle leaves the racket of the server during the service. The ability to correctly judge the trajectory, direction and drop point of an incoming stroke is essential.

Repositioning and Setting Up the Racket

Moving and quickly repositioning to the proper spot to get ready for the incoming stroke is the foundation of all offensive strategies in badminton. During the repositioning, the player should be able to not only relocate himself or herself in a prompt manner, but to also remain balanced and move the racket into the proper position for the execution of the returning stroke. To set up the shot, the player usually positions the racket in a direction that is completely opposite to that of the racket swing.

Arriving, Executing the Stroke and Returning to the Center of the Court

It is extremely critical for the player to control his or her balance. The knees need to be bent slightly once the feet land on the court. The power necessary to return the shuttle comes not only from the swing of the racket and the snapping motion of the wrist, but also from the body movement. Regardless of whether it is a forehand or a backhand stroke, in order to produce the greatest force at the point of contact, the player should accumulate all possible energy from the motion of the entire body. As soon as the back swing begins, the player should turn the body to facilitate the arm's movement, eventually transferring all the power to the snapping motion at the wrist. A successful stroke involves the harmonized motions of all the body parts: the legs, the torso, the arms, and the wrist. The ultimate goal of each stroke is to produce the greatest impact between the racket and the shuttle at the moment of contact so that the shuttle will be returned to the opponent's side of the court with a certain velocity, power and angle.

After each stroke, the player should immediately relax the arm, withdraw the racket, hold the racket in front of the body and prepare for the next action. The player does not always have to return immediately to the center of the court after each stroke. He or she may move from where the last shot was taken to take the next shot.

Chapter 6

Fundamentals in Badminton

Gripping the Racket

Gripping the racket is one of the most important techniques to master before learning other badminton skills. The way to grip the racket depends on specific situations. The player may use a different grip to hit the shuttle coming from certain angles or to return the shuttle to a specific area. Players with diverse technical styles may also choose different grips while completing the same movement. A sound grip helps a player to successfully execute various badminton techniques.

In general, there are two common ways to grip a badminton racket: the forehand grip and the backhand grip. For the consistency of the description of various techniques, the right hand is the dominant hand of the player in this book.

The Forehand Grip

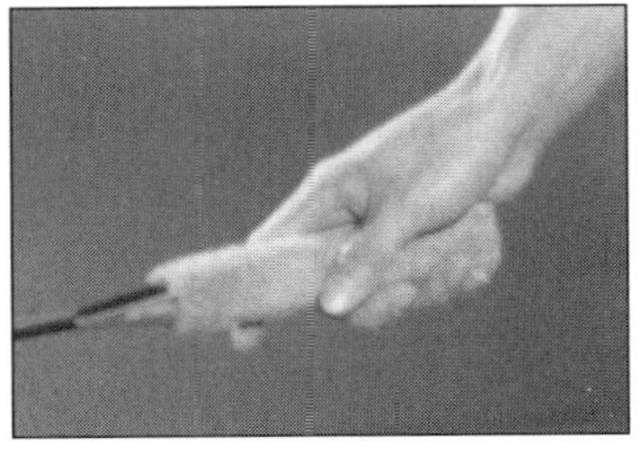

Figure 6.1.1: The forehand grip

Holding the racket with the forehand grip is similar to shaking hands with a friend. The thumb and the forefinger should form a V-shape and be placed on the left top small facet of the handle. The thumb and the forefinger may then rest on the right and left big facets of the handle, respectively. The rest of the fingers are spread around the handle. (See Figures 6.1.1 and 6.1.2.) The player should not hold the racket too tight. Some space should be left between the palm and the racket. The racket face should be perpendicular to the court floor when the arm is extended forward. The forehand grip is used for forehand serves, strokes from the player's right

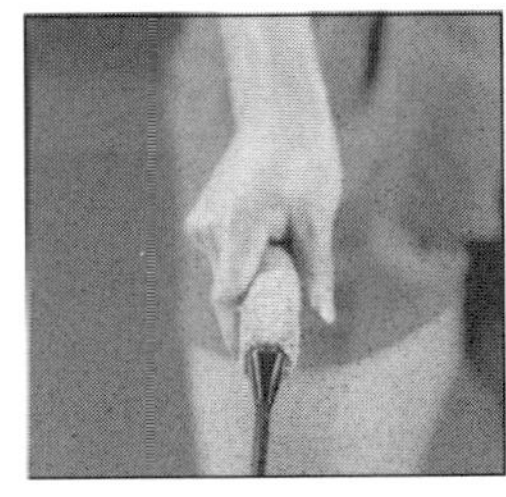

Figure 6.1.2: The forehand grip

side of the court and round-the-head shots from the left side of the player.

The Backhand Grip

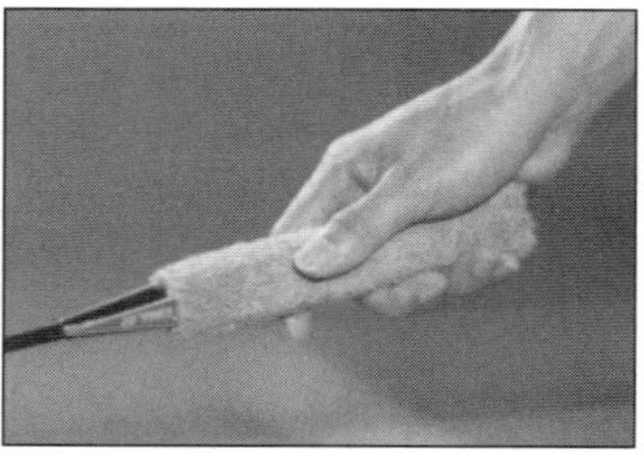

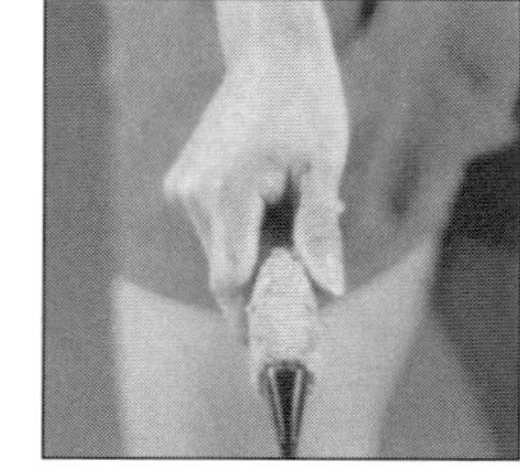

Figure 6.2.1 and 6.2.2: The backhand grip

The backhand grip is used when striking a shuttle with such techniques as the backhand serve, the backhand drive, and the backhand clear. From the forehand grip, the player uses the thumb and the forefinger to turn the handle clockwise. The thumb is placed flat on either the left big facet or the top left small facet of the handle. The rest of the fingers are spread around the handle. Again, there should be a little space between the palm and the racket. (See Figure 6.2.1 and Figure 6.2.2.) Generally speaking, to utilize the backhand grip the player should turn the body either sideways to the left or halfway around with the back facing the opponent.

Positioning on the Court

The Ready Positions

The ready position refers to the special stance that a player takes after he or she completes a shot and returns to the center of the court in singles or respective position in doubles.

The Ready Position in Singles

In general, it is essential that the player return to the center of the court after each shot. This area is commonly referred to as the "home base." In the ready position, both knees are bent slightly, the feet are separated shoulder-width apart with the center of gravity falling between them, the dominant foot is placed in front and the upper body is leaned slightly forward. The player holds the racket in front of the body. (See Figure 6.3.1—front view and Figure 6.3.2—side view.)

Figure 6.3.1: Ready position (front view)

Figure 6.3.2: Ready position (side view)

The Ready Position in Doubles

The ready position in doubles is similar to the one in singles. (See Figure 6.4.) After each shot, the player should return to a designated area and assume the ready position. The location of this designated area is determined by several factors to be discussed in Chapter 11.

Figure 6.4: Ready position in doubles

Positions for Service Reception

The position for service reception refers to the stance that the player takes for receiving the serve and the location where the player stands. It is crucial for a player to properly position himself or herself to receive the serve.

The Position for Service Reception in Singles

The position that a player takes for service reception in singles varies depending on where the shuttle is served. As mentioned earlier, the server always delivers the shuttle diagonally; that is, from right service court to right service court and from left service court to left service court.

When receiving the serve, the receiver first needs to choose a proper ready position and stance. In general, the ready position for singles is about 5 feet away from the short service line and close to the center line if the serve is released from the right service court. If the player is about to receive a serve from the left service court, the receiver should be in the middle area between the center line and the left sideline. This position allows the player to cover the court for both short or long serves. For a left-handed player, the position for service reception is opposite from the one for a right-handed player. That means, the player should stand in the middle area between the center line and the right sideline to receive the serve from the right

Figure 6.5: Stance for service reception in singles

service court, and should stand near the center line on the left service court to receive a serve from the left service court.

To assume the ready stance for receiving the serve in singles, the player positions his or her feet apart with the left foot in front and the right in rear. The body is sideways toward the net. The center of gravity is over the left foot and the right heel is raised slightly. The racket is held naturally in front of the body. (See Figure 6.5.)

The Position for Service Reception in Doubles

The position for receiving the serve in doubles is similar to the one used in singles, except it is closer to the short service line because the length of a doubles court is shorter than that of a singles court during the service. The doubles player should prepare to receive a short serve.

The stance for service reception in doubles is the same except for two differences. The player may place his or her center of gravity over either the front or the rear foot, or in between the two feet. The racket should be held high above the shoulders. (See Figure 6.6.)

Figure 6.6: Stance for service reception in doubles

Fundamental Footwork

In addition to mastering various basic techniques and strokes, it is essential for a player to utilize skilled footwork. Footwork is a set of footsteps that a player uses to move on the court. Whether or not a player can move quickly and accurately on the court depends on how adept the player is in utilizing the fundamental footwork. There are three types of fundamental footwork: footwork for underhand strokes, footwork for overhead strokes, and footwork for sideward movement. Each type generally starts from the center of the court. Figure 6.7 illustrates the moving direction of these three particular patterns of footwork.

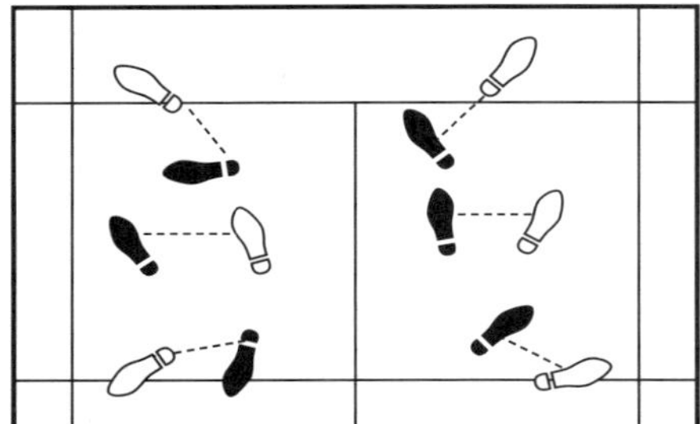

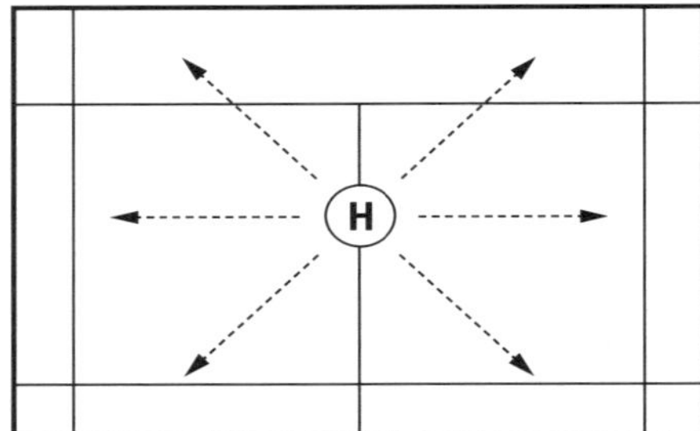

H = "Home" Position

Figure 6.7: Patterns of fundamental footwork

Start, move, stop and hit, and return are the four basic elements of any type of footwork. To achieve the most efficient footwork, there are two important points to remember. First, most of the time the dominant foot (e.g., the right foot for the right-handed player) should be placed as the last step in any type of footwork prior to striking. Second, both the ready position as well as the position for service reception affects the effectiveness of a specific type of footwork.

The Footwork for Underhand Strokes

The footwork for most of the underhand strokes (to be described in detail in the next chapter) is virtually the same. Depending on the distance between the player and the point where the shuttle drops, the player may apply either a two-step or three-step footwork pattern. If the player is close to the shuttle, he or she may choose the two-step pattern. Otherwise, the three-step pattern should be used.

<u>Footwork for the Forehand Underhand Strokes</u>

There usually are two movement patterns of footwork for forehand underhand strokes; the two-step movement pattern and the three-step movement pattern. The two-step pattern is quite simple. The player first moves the left foot across the body toward the front right court, and then moves the right foot following the same movement pattern. (See Figure 6.8.1.)

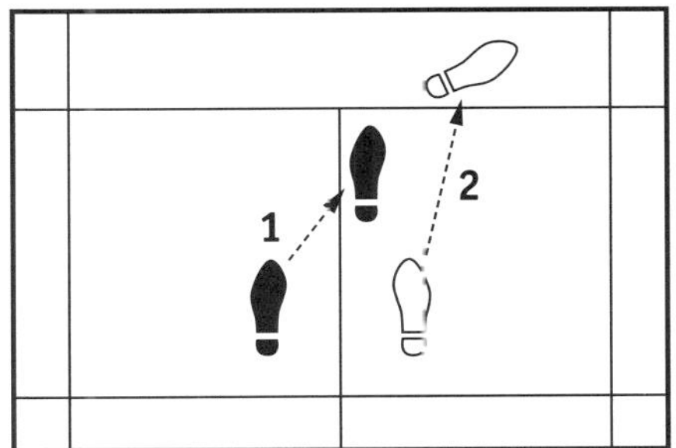

Figure 6.8.1: Two-step pattern

There are two ways to apply the three-step pattern. The first one is shown in Figure 6.8.2. The player starts by moving the right foot a half step toward the front right court, followed by the two-step pattern.

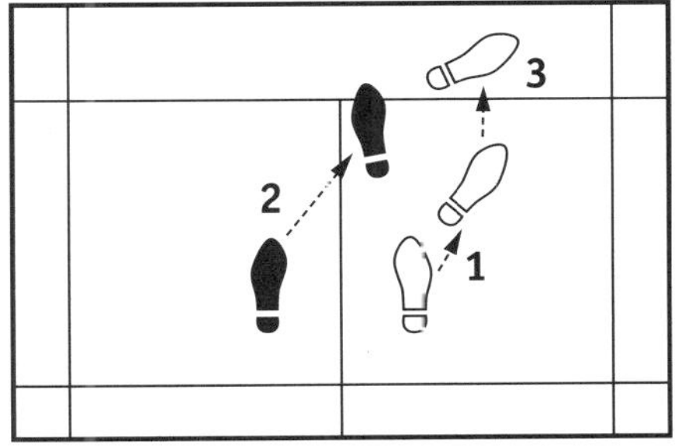

Figure 6.8.2: Three-step pattern

In a variation of the three-step pattern, the player may take a half step forward with the right foot, and then move the left foot following behind the heel of the right foot. Immediately after this movement, the player launches the body forward with power generated from the left foot, and at the same time, thrusts the right foot with a big step and the toes pointed toward the shuttle. Figure 6.8.3 illustrates this type of three-step pattern. The center of gravity is located approximately one-third of the distance between the right heel and the left toes. The bigger the step, the closer the center of gravity will be to the right heel.

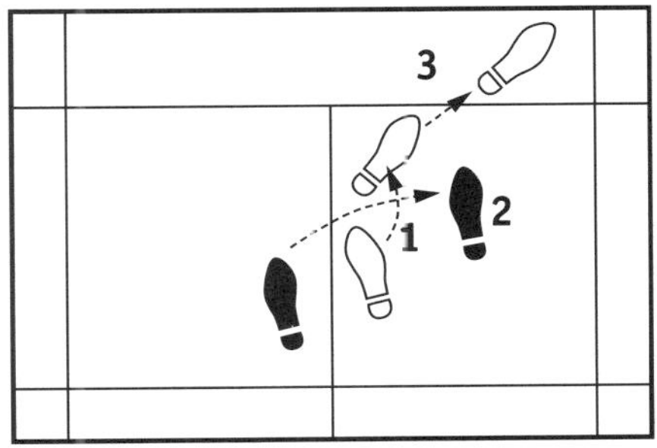

Figure 6.8.3: Three-step pattern (variation)

Footwork for Backhand Underhand Strokes

The footwork for the backhand underhand strokes is almost exactly the same as those of the forehand underhand strokes. The only difference is in the direction of movement.

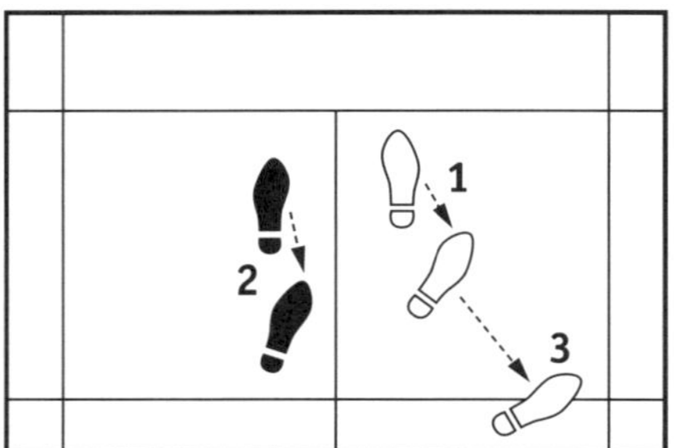

Figure 6.9.1: Overhead stroke footwork

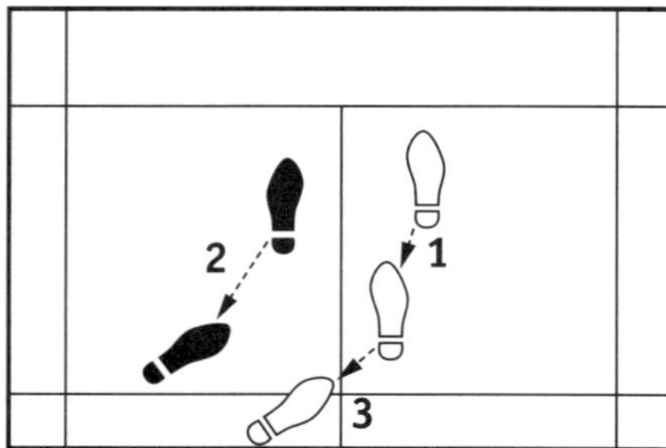

Figure 6.9.2: The running pattern

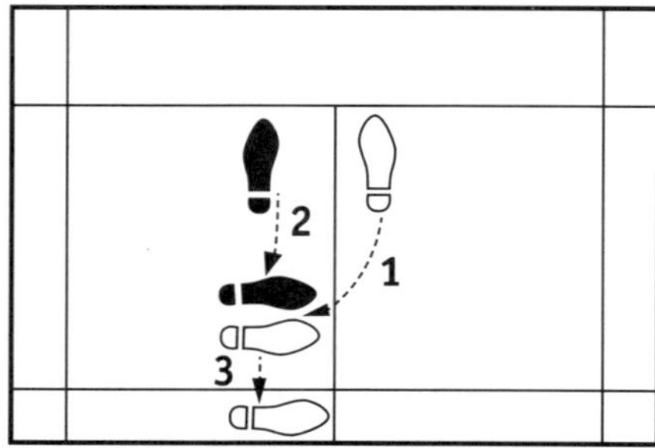

Figure 6.9.3: The slide pattern

Footwork for Overhead Strokes

The footwork for overhead strokes includes those for the forehand overhead strokes and those for the backhand overhead strokes. Regardless of the type of footwork used for overhead strokes, the player should always keep his or her eyes on the incoming shuttle while maneuvering the body backward.

To perform the footwork for the forehand overhead strokes, the player first moves the front foot backward and turns the body sideward from the ready position, with the left side of the body facing the net. (See Figure 6.9.1.) From that position, the player may either run (see Figure 6.9.2) or slide (see Figure 6.9.3) backward to retreat to the targeted spot. Both patterns can be used to execute the stroke from the back of the left court or the back of the right court.

There are two types of footwork used for the backhand overhead strokes. The first is the two-step pattern, in which the player steps backward and sideward with the left foot followed by the crossover of the right foot. This movement also facilitates the rotation of the trunk. Once the footwork is concluded, the back of the player should completely face the net and the toe of the right foot (the hitting foot) should point toward the left backhand corner. The feet are staggered with the hitting foot forward. The player's center of gravity should then be over the right leg that is bent slightly at the knee joint. (See Figure 6.9.4.)

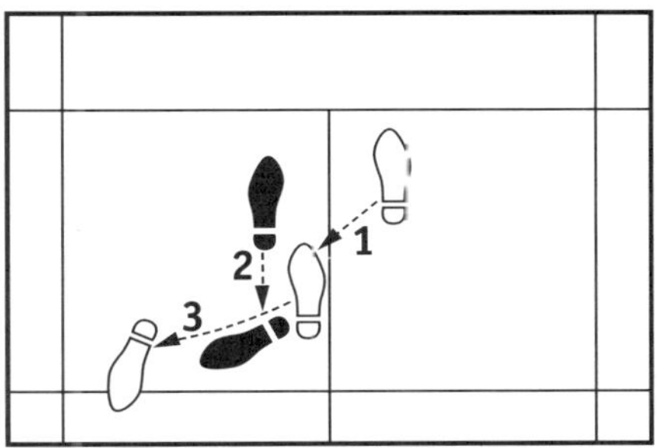

Figure 6.9.4: Conclusion of overhead stroke footwork

The second type of footwork for the backhand overhead is the three-step pattern. In the three-step pattern, the player starts by withdrawing the front foot backward, behind the left foot, and then moves the left and right feet backward sequentially. Similar to the two-step pattern, the player crosses the right foot over and in front of the left foot. As a result of this crossover motion, the player's back faces the net.

Footwork for Sideward or Lateral Movements

Sideward or lateral movements are used most frequently to return the opponent's offensive strokes, such as smashes and quick drop shots, that fall near the side lines. The player may take one or two lateral steps to the intended area. To execute the one-step pattern, the player takes a big step laterally with either the right or left foot, depending on where the shuttle is coming from and drops. If the drop point is too far away for the player to stride with a big step, the player should use the two-step pattern.

There are two common two-step patterns. Figure 6.10.1 demonstrates the first pattern used to move to the left-hand side. From the ready position, the player moves the right foot across and behind the left foot. As soon as the right foot lands, the player drives the body with the right leg toward the left sideline and steps out on the left foot. In the second two-step pattern for

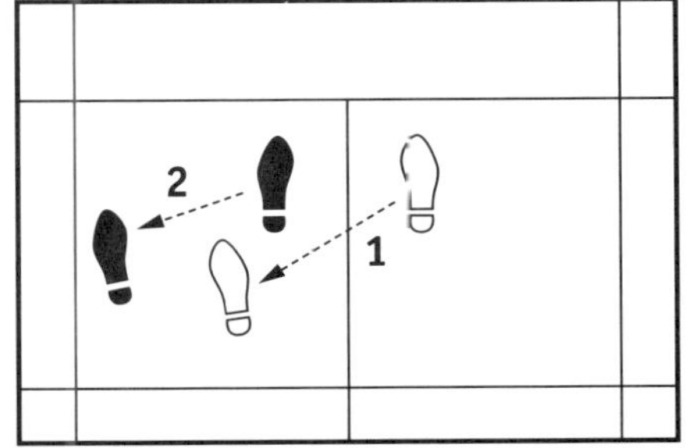

Figure 6.10.1: Lateral footwork to the left (first variation)

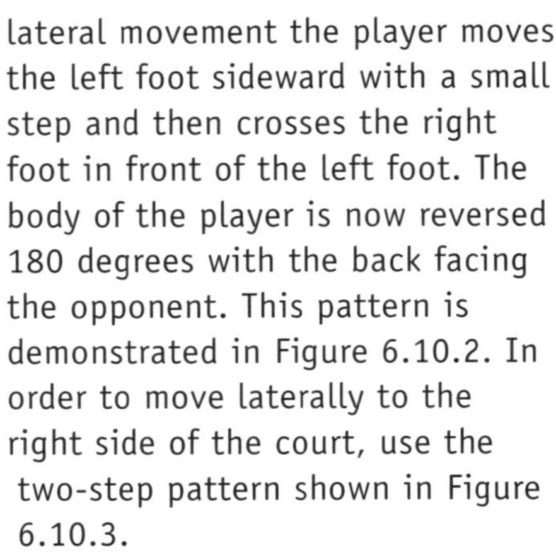

lateral movement the player moves the left foot sideward with a small step and then crosses the right foot in front of the left foot. The body of the player is now reversed 180 degrees with the back facing the opponent. This pattern is demonstrated in Figure 6.10.2. In order to move laterally to the right side of the court, use the two-step pattern shown in Figure 6.10.3.

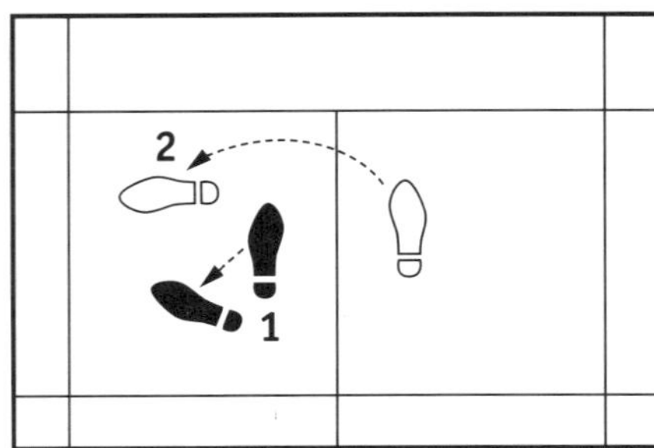

Figure 6.10.2: Lateral footwork to the left (second variation)

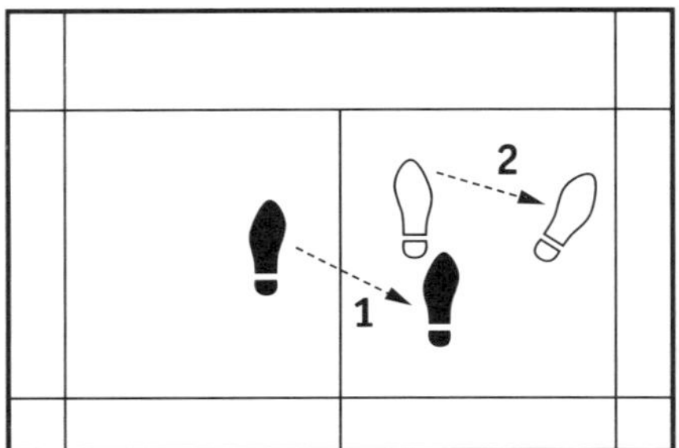

Figure 6.10.3: Lateral footwork to the right

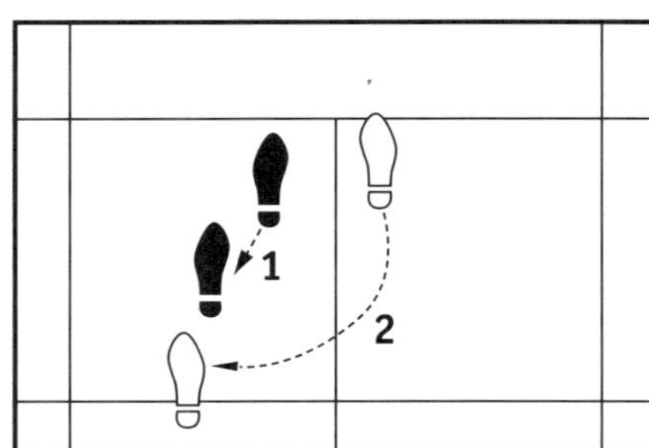

Figure 6.11: Round-the-head stroke footwork

<u>Footwork for the Round-the-Head Stroke</u>

The round-the-head stroke is most often used to return a shuttle that is hit toward the left back court and above the left shoulder. (See Figure 6.11.) From the ready position, the player moves the left foot slightly backward and sideward. Then the player moves the right foot back diagonally, crossing the back of the left foot, and strikes the shuttle.

Chapter 7

The Forehand Strokes

There are many different ways to return the shuttle in badminton, including overhead clears, smashes, drop shots, underhand clears and push shots. All of these techniques can be executed with either the forehand stroke or the backhand stroke. This chapter discusses the forehand strokes. The forehand strokes consist of the forehand overhead strokes, the forehand underhand strokes and the forehand drive.

The Forehand Overhead Strokes

The forehand overhead strokes are used when the shuttle is hit high above the head. The three types of forehand overhead strokes are the overhead clear, the smash and the drop shot. Technically, there are many similarities among these three strokes. As a result, the player should attempt to execute them in a consistent fashion. This will confuse the opponent.

The Forehand Overhead Clear

The forehand overhead clear is a technique used to return the shuttle to the opponent's deep backcourt. Depth and height are two basic elements of the stroke. To execute the forehand overhead clear, the player must first determine from where the shuttle is coming (direction) and where it will drop. Then the player quickly turns the body to the side and moves to the spot where the shuttle may fall in front and above his or her right shoulder. The left shoulder of the player is toward the net with the left foot in front and the center of gravity placed above the right foot. The left arm is raised and bent at the elbow. The racket is held up above the right shoulder. The forehand overhead clear is executed with the backward movement of the right forearm and the racket as a whole unit. The right elbow is elevated. The racket is directly behind the head at this point. The player then extends the elbow and quickly and forcefully throws the forearm upward with power generated from the extension of the rear foot and the rotation of the torso. The shuttle should contact the racket right above the right shoulder when the arm is fully extended. After contact, the player shifts his or her body weight to the front foot and follows through with the racket to the left side of the body. (See Figures 7.1.1 through 7.1.4.)

Figure 7.1.1

Figure 7.1.2

Figure 7.1.3

Figure 7.1.4

Figures 7.1.1 through 7.1.4: The forehand overhead clear

The Forehand Smash

The forehand smash is a shot that forcefully returns the shuttle at its highest point with a downward trajectory. It is one of the major offensive techniques. The smash has several categories based on the amount of force applied to the stroke. These include the heavy smash (with substantial amount of force), the light smash (with little amount of force), and the point smash (with modest amount of force and the shuttle landing very close to the net). The smash can also be classified based on the length of its trajectory: the long smash (with the landing point far away from the net) and the short smash (with the landing point close to the net).

Technically speaking, the entire technique of the forehand smash approximates that of the forehand overhead clear prior to the contact. Nevertheless, several differences should be noted. First, the player should attempt to contact the shuttle in front of the body, not above the shoulder. Second, the effectiveness of a smash relies on the amount of force that can be generated from the snapping motion of the wrist. Therefore, the quicker the player unlocks the wrist and the more force involved in the downward swing, the more momentum generated in the stroke and the more powerful the smash will be. (See Figures 7.2.1, 7.2.2, 7.2.3 and Figures 7.2.4 and 7.2.5 on the next page.)

Figures 7.2.1, 7.2.3 and 7.2.3: The forehand smash

Figures 7.2.4 and 7.2.5: Completion of the forehand smash

The Forehand Drop Shots

The drop shot is a shot that is hit from back court, barely clears the net and drops to the opponent's front court. There are two types of forehand drop shots, based on the flying speed and where the shuttle drops: the quick (or chopping) drop shot and the light (or blocking) drop shot . Again the shuttle is contacted, the player should begin the forehand drop shot in the same way as the overhead clear and smash.

<u>The Quick Drop Shot</u>

To perform the quick drop shot the player should turn the racket sideways prior to contacting the shuttle and quickly hit the shuttle at the back and right side of the base with a chopping-like downward motion. To make a quick drop shot from the right back court to the opponent's right front court, the player should make the contact only on the right side of the base and snap the wrist toward the left and downward.

<u>The Light Drop Shot</u>

There are two ways to execute the light drop shot. One is similar to the quick drop shot. At the point of contact, the player decelerates, controls the wrist motion, and hits the shuttle softly. The other way to perform the light drop shot is to block the shuttle and use the reaction force to bounce it back to the opponent's front court close to the net. This technique is often used to intercept the opponent's attacking overhead clear (an overhead clear with a flat trajectory).

Figures 7.3.1, 7.3.2 and 7.3.3: The forehand round-the-head shot

The Forehand Round-the-Head Shot

The forehand round-the-head shot, shown in Figures 7.3.1, 7.3.2 and 7.3.3, is a type of special forehand overhead stroke. It is often used with the forehand overhead technique to hit a shuttle that is falling over and above the left shoulder. The player executes the shot by bending his or her back and knees toward the left back corner of the court with the body primarily facing the net. The player then swings the racket around the left-hand shoulder. The player can use the forehand round-the-head technique to execute many shots, including the clear, drop shot and smash. It is strongly recommended that a beginner use the round-the-head shot before attempting to utilize the backhand overhead techniques. There are several reasons for this. First, the forehand overhead strokes normally are much more powerful than the backhand overhead strokes. Second, it is difficult for beginning badminton players to execute the backhand overhead techniques effectively. Third, it is easier to control the dropping point with the forehand overhead techniques than the backhand techniques.

The Forehand Underhand Strokes

The forehand underhand techniques include the forehand underhand clear, the forehand push shot and the forehand underhand net plays. The technique for the forehand underhand net plays will be explained in Chapter 10.

Figures 7.4.1, 7.4.2 and 7.4.3: The forehand underhand clear

The Forehand Underhand Clear

The forehand underhand clear is a defensive technique used to return the shuttle from the forehand front court below the net to the opponent's back court with a high flying trajectory. The player begins the forehand underhand clear with a stride step (the toes of the right foot pointed at the shuttle and the center of gravity between the front and rear feet). The racket is held in front of the body and the arm bent slightly at the elbow. The player bends the wrist, swings the racket downwards, forwards and upwards, and snaps the wrist. There is little forearm involvement in the movement. The power comes primarily from the quick snapping motion of the wrist. (See Figures 7.4.1, 7.4.2 and 7.4.3.)

The Forehand Push Shot

The push shot is usually executed near the net to hit the shuttle to the opponent's back court with a low, flat trajectory, and a relatively fast speed. It is a very effective offensive technique. The way the forehand underhand push shot is executed is similar to that of the forehand underhand clear with four exceptions. First, the point of contact made with the shuttle in the push shot is higher than that of the underhand clear, usually about one foot below the top of the net. Second, the racket is swung with a slight downward and primarily forward movement. There is no upward motion involved. Third, the snapping movement of the wrist is obvious and drastic. Fourth, the elbow is slightly bent during the back swing and extended as the wrist

Figures 7.5.1, 7.5.2 and 7.5.3: The forehand push shot

snaps. The forearm is rotated inwards and accompanied with the forward movement of the racket-hand-arm unit. (See Figures 7.5.1, 7.5.2 and 7.5.3.)

The Forehand Drive

The forehand drive is a common technique used, especially in doubles, to regain offensive control of the play. It is usually executed when the shuttle is coming low and fast to the right side of the player. The shuttle is hit forcefully so that it returns fast in a flat path.

To perform this technique, the player places the right foot toward the right sideline and at the same time turns the body to face the incoming shuttle. Then, the player raises both the forearm and racket together as a unit beside the body and swings backward. The wrist should pivot gradually during this backward movement. After that, the player throws the forearm/racket unit quickly and forcefully forward and rolls the wrist toward the shuttle. The power of the movement comes from the quick forearm forward swing and the wrist snap. (See Figures 7.6.1 through 7.6.4 on the next page.)

Figure 7.6.1

Figure 7.6.2

Figure 7.6.3

Figure 7.6.4

Figures 7.6.1 through 7.6.4: The forehand drive

Chapter 8

The Backhand Strokes

Similar to the forehand strokes, the backhand strokes also have three major categories: the backhand overhead strokes, the backhand underhand strokes and the backhand drive.

The Backhand Overhead Strokes

The backhand overhead strokes include the backhand overhead clear, the backhand smash and the backhand drop shot. The body and arm movement and the footwork of these three types of backhand overhead strokes are almost identical with slight differences found only in the point of contact and the amount of force. After making the decision to use the backhand overhead stroke the player should quickly change the grip to the backhand grip. While changing the grip, the player may apply either the two-step or the three-step pattern for backhand overhead strokes to relocate to the target spot. The player pulls the racket toward the chest with the right elbow raised to about shoulder height and the forearm rotated inward. The wrist is abducted. It is the authors' belief that the backhand overhead strokes are the most difficult of all the badminton techniques.

The Backhand Overhead Clear

The backhand overhead clear begins with a slight extension of the right knee to generate an upward movement of the player's center of gravity. This extension also helps the player elevate the point of contact. The trunk continues the upward movement initiated by the extension of the right leg. As the player raises up the trunk, he or she also rotates the trunk clockwise. The player initiates the forward swing from the upper arm by extending the elbow and then forearm. The stroke is completed with an adducting action of the right wrist. There is no follow-through movement. Again, the player should make contact with the shuttle when the racket is as high as possible above the shoulder. (See Figures 8.1.1, 8.1.2 and 8.1.3.)

Figure 8.1.1, 8.1.2 and 8.1.3: The backhand overhead clear

The Backhand Smash

In general, the technique of the backhand smash is similar to that of the backhand overhead clear. The footwork, body and arm movements are the same. There are two main differences: the point of contact and the power of the snapping motion. For an effective attack and offensive angle, the player should choose a point of contact that is located behind the body or several inches back from the point of contact for the backhand overhead clear (remember that the player's back is now facing the net). The shuttle should be contacted at the highest point possible. When performing the smash, regardless of whether it is the forehand or backhand, power is very important. More power must be applied to strike the shuttle in the backhand overhead smash than in the backhand overhead clear. That means the player needs to snap the wrist much more forcefully and faster.

The Backhand Drop Shot

As mentioned previously, the three types of backhand overhead strokes are almost identical in terms of footwork and body and arm movement with the only differences in the point of impact and the use of force. The backhand drop shot shares a common point of contact with the backhand smash. Prior to contacting the shuttle, the player needs to control the amount of wrist adduction. Similar to the forehand drop shot, the shuttle should be hit at the back and left side of the base with a chopping-like downward motion. Again, there is no follow-through movement.

The Backhand Underhand Strokes

As with the forehand underhand strokes, the backhand underhand strokes are also used to return shots coming to the left side of the player and near the net. To properly execute the backhand underhand strokes, the backhand grip is required. Once the judgment has been made that the opponent's shot will drop close to the net on the left side of the court, the player should quickly point the racket toward the left side and turn the body to face the shuttle. Either the two-step or the three-step pattern for backhand underhand strokes can be utilized. The backhand underhand strokes include the clear, the push shot and the net play. The backhand underhand net play is described in Chapter 10.

The Backhand Underhand Clear

To perform the backhand underhand clear, the player first bends the elbow slightly and abducts the wrist. This is followed by swinging the racket downwards, forwards and upwards. The shuttle is hit with a quick adducting motion of the wrist. There should not be any noticeable shoulder movement. The motion involves only the elbow, the forearm and the wrist. The shuttle should be hit so that it flies high and lands near the back boundary line. (See Figures 8.2.1, 8.2.2 and 8.2.3.)

The Backhand Push Shot

The backhand push shot is executed from the left side of the body near the net. The shuttle is contacted at a point that is just below the net. It is used to return a shot with a low, flat trajectory. To initiate the

Figure 8.2.1, 8.2.2 and 8.2.3: The backhand underhand clear

technique, the player brings the racket backward with the elbow bent slightly and the wrist abducted. The player then pushes the racket forcefully forward by extending the elbow, rotating the forearm outward and snapping the wrist. (See Figure 8.3.1, 8.3.2 and 8.3.3.)

Figure 8.3.1, 8.3.2 and 8.3.3: The backhand push shot

The Backhand Drive

The backhand drive is a technique with similar offensive merits of the forehand drive. It is commonly used in doubles. Again, the player must use the backhand grip to ensure the effectiveness of this particular stroke.

Proper execution of the backhand drive requires the player to bring the racket to the left side of the body quickly with the elbow flexed and wrist abducted. As the player brings the racket to the left, he or she should turn the upper body to face the left net post. Power is generated from the quick extension of the forearm at the elbow and adduction of the wrist. (See Figure 8.4.1, 8.4.2 and 8.4.3.)

Figures 8.4.1, 8.4.2 and 8.4.3: The backhand drive

Chapter 9

The Service and Reception

The Service

Each point of play starts with a serve. A serve is a stroke that the server uses to hit the shuttle to the receiver's court. The serve is an integral part of game strategy, because the quality of a serve can directly place the server into either an offensive position or a defensive position, ultimately affecting the outcome of the play—by either scoring a point or losing the serve. There are two basic rules governing the serve. The entire head of the racket should be below the hand gripping the handle and no higher than waist level. Details on rules related to the serve can be found in Chapter 4 and the Appendix: Laws of Badminton. Contact with the shuttle must be made while the wrist is rolled and snapped. There are two types of serves, the forehand serve and the backhand serve.

The Forehand Serves

All serves delivered from the forehand side are forehand serves. Based on variations in flying paths, the forehand serves can be divided into four categories: the deep serve, the flat deep serve, the drive serve and the short serve.

To perform the forehand serve, the player stands with the feet shoulder-width apart and the left shoulder facing the opponent. The left foot is in front pointed forward. The right foot is behind pointed to the right sideline. The center of gravity is over the rear (right) foot. It is required that part of both feet remain in contact with the court until the serve is made. In general, the shuttle is held at the base with the thumb, the forefinger and the middle finger of the left hand in front of the body about chest high. The left arm is extended and bent slightly at the elbow. The racket arm is raised laterally on the right side of the body with the elbow bent slightly. The preparatory phase and forward swing for all types of forehand serves are identical.

Figure 9.1: Ready position for the forehand serve

The difference is in how the shuttle is hit and the follow-through movement. (See Figure 9.1.)

<u>The Forehand Deep Serve</u>

The forehand deep serve is most frequently used to initiate play in singles. It is usually made from a spot that is about two to three feet away from the short service line. The player should keep part of both feet on the floor until the serve is completed. From the ready position for serving, the player swings the racket downwards and forwards with the forearm moving ahead of the wrist, which is gradually extended during the forward swing. As the forward swing commences, the player drops the shuttle. The player flexes the wrist immediately prior to impact, so that power can be generated at the point of contact. The center of gravity is gradually shifted from the rear foot to the front foot during the completion of the forward swing. After hitting the shuttle, the player moves the racket forward and upward to complete the follow through. A properly executed forehand deep serve should send the shuttle high and far into the opponent's deep court near the back boundary line. (See Figures 9.2.1 through 9.2.4.)

Figure 9.2.1

Figure 9.2.2

Figure 9.2.3

Figure 9.2.4

Figures 9.2.1 through 9.2.4: The forehand deep serve

The Forehand Flat Deep Serve

The entire motion and technique of the forehand flat deep serve is almost identical to the forehand deep serve, the only difference being the moment of contact. While snapping the wrist, the player applies the force more forward and upward at the point of contact. This causes the shuttle to fly lower than when hit with the forehand deep serve, but still be high enough to be blocked by the opponent. Because of its quick and low course, it is difficult for the opponent to have sufficient time to react to this serve.

Figure 9.3.1, 9.3.2 and 9.3.3: The forehand drive serve

The Forehand Drive Serve

Low trajectory and fast speed characterize the forehand drive serve. It is usually used to catch the opponent by surprise, because it is targeted at the area right above the left shoulder or the so-called "off-racket" shoulder of the opponent. A very fast wrist flex or quick snapping motion at the wrist is the key for a successful forehand drive serve. (See Figures 9.3.1, 9.3.2 and 9.3.3.)

The Forehand Short Serve

While executing the forehand short serve, the player deliberately controls the wrist and the force applied to the shuttle. The shuttle is hit in such a soft manner that it barely clears the net and lands near the short service line. The short serve is commonly used in doubles. Sometimes, players in singles also utilize it to keep his or her opponent off-guard. In order to be effective when using the forehand short serve, the player needs to have good control of the racket and the wrist. Keep the wrist extended at the point of contact (i.e., no snapping motion at the wrist) with very little follow-through. (See Figures 9.4.1, 9.4.2 and 9.4.3.)

Figure 9.5 depicts the trajectories of the four types of forehand serves.

Figures 9.4.1, 9.4.2 and 9.4.3: The forehand short serve

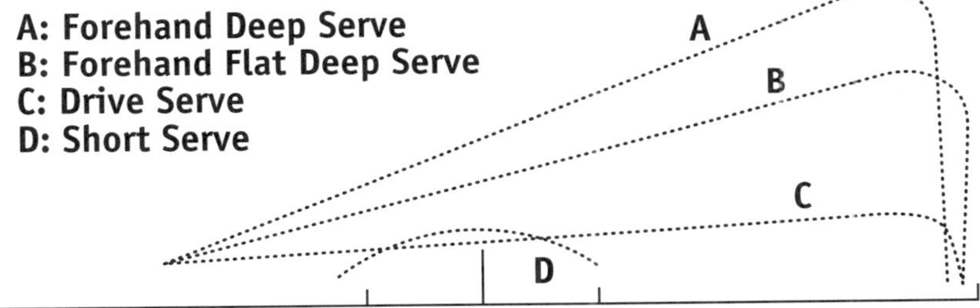

Figure 9.5: Trajectories of the four types of forehand serves

The Backhand Serves

Because it is much less effective than the forehand deep serve, no backhand deep serve is used. Other than that, the backhand flat deep serve, the backhand drive serve and the backhand short serve are the three most common backhand service techniques. These serves are used primarily in doubles.

Again, the stance and the preparation phase of these three types of backhand serves are basically the same. Differences are in the use of force and in the follow-through phase. The player uses a reverse stance (i.e., the right foot in front with toes pointing forward) and the

Figure 9.6.1, 9.6.2 and 9.6.3: The backhand serve

backhand grip in the execution of all of the backhand serves. Standing near the short service line and placing the body weight over the front foot, the player holds the racket in front of the body with the head of the racket pointing downward and the elbow slightly raised. The player should hold the shuttle by the feathers with the thumb and forefinger so that the base of the shuttle points toward the right side. To execute a backhand serve, the player first moves the racket backward laterally, and then swings it back. The player releases the shuttle immediately before the racket contacts it. The shuttle should be hit at about waist height. (See Figures 9.6.1, 9.6.2 and 9.6.3.)

<u>The Backhand Flat Deep Serve</u>

The backhand flat deep serve shares the same trajectory and offensive merits of the forehand flat deep serve. When using the flat deep serve, the opponent usually has less time to react to the serve and to formulate a thoughtful returning tactic. At the point of contact, the player quickly snaps the wrist so that the shuttle will fly primarily forward and upward.

<u>The Backhand Short Serve</u>

Control is the key for the effective use of the backhand short serve. As soon as the forward swing begins, the player turns the racket slightly counterclockwise so that the racket will contact the shuttle with a slicing, controlled fashion. No snapping motion should be used while executing the backhand short serve. The entire movement is controlled at the elbow. Again, as mentioned earlier, both the forehand

and backhand short serves are frequently used in doubles. Therefore, it is critical that the shuttle barely crosses the net and drops past but near the front service line.

The Backhand Drive Serve

The backhand drive serve utilizes a forceful adducting action. This serve is used in both singles and doubles to catch the opponent off-guard. It should not be used as a regular serving strategy. The backhand drive serve has a long, low flat trajectory, angled toward the back court, which is similar to the forehand drive serve.

Reception

The Ready Position

The ready position for returning the serve for both singles and doubles is a modification of the ready position used during a rally, which was discussed in Chapter 6. (See Figure 9.7.) When receiving a serve, the player places his or her feet comfortably apart with the left foot ahead of the right foot in a diagonal stance. This position enables the receiver to move forward or backward depending on the type of serve hit by the opponent. After taking the ready position to receive a serve, the receiver must keep both of his or her feet stationary until the server's racket contacts the shuttle. (See Chapter 6 for more details about positions for service reception.)

Figure 9.7: The ready position for receiving the serve

Receiving

The anticipation of the direction of a serve is critical for an effective return. The receiver needs to adjust his or her position accordingly and shift the body weight in the direction of the serve in order to get a good start of the rally. Over-anticipation, however, can give the server the opportunity to catch the receiver off-guard with a change in direction or depth of the serve.

Chapter 10

The Net Plays

The net plays refer to the strokes players make near the net. These shots typically have short trajectories and barely clear the net. In general, a badminton player should attempt to master at least three basic net play techniques: the net drop shot, the cross-net drop shot and the net smash.

The Forehand Net Plays

The Forehand Net Drop

The forehand net drop is a soft, low, underhand shot that is made close to the net from the right side of the body. The shuttle is hit so gently that it barely clears the net and lands in the opponent's forecourt. Because of its short and low trajectory, this type of stroke is also called a "hairpin drop." While executing the forehand net drop, the player should hold the racket face parallel to the floor and as close to net height as possible. The higher the point of contact made, the more offensive the shot will be. Before making a forehand net drop, the player should assume a stride step like the one used to execute other underhand strokes (e.g., the underhand clear). The shuttle should be hit gently at arm's length in front of the body. The player cocks the wrist slightly and brings the racket backward, followed by a controlled, soft snapping motion so that the shuttle will immediately drop down once it clears the net. (See Figures 10.1.1 and 10.1.2.)

Figures 10.1.1 and 10.1.2: The forehand net drop

In a more advanced version of the forehand net drop, the player can actually make the shuttle roll or whirl over the net along the transverse axis of the shuttle. The faster the shuttle rolls, the harder it is for the opponent to return it. This is achieved when the player slices the base of the shuttle with the racket. The forearm is slightly rotated outward during the slicing motion. The key for a fine execution of any net drop is control in the use of force and control in the angle formed by the racket face and the floor. The force applied to the racket depends on the position of the incoming shuttle and its speed. An improper hitting angle may cause either failure to hit the shuttle over the net or the return to be too high, jeopardizing the player's offensive position.

The Forehand Cross-Net Drop

Another forehand net play technique is the forehand cross-net drop. In this technique the shuttle is hit across the net and lands on the opposite side of the opponent's front court. The initial phase of this technique is the same as the one of the forehand net drop, in which the player, with a strike step, holds the racket up and in front of the body and cocks the wrist slightly. From that position, the player immediately changes the grip by rotating the racket clockwise so that the thumb is on the left big facet of the racket handle. Next, the player quickly flexes the forearm and wrist slightly at both the elbow and wrist joints, accompanied by a small inward motion in the forearm as well as in the wrist. The quality of the execution of this shot depends on how well the player can control the racket face and application of force. (See Figures 10.2.1, 10.2.2 and 10.2.3.)

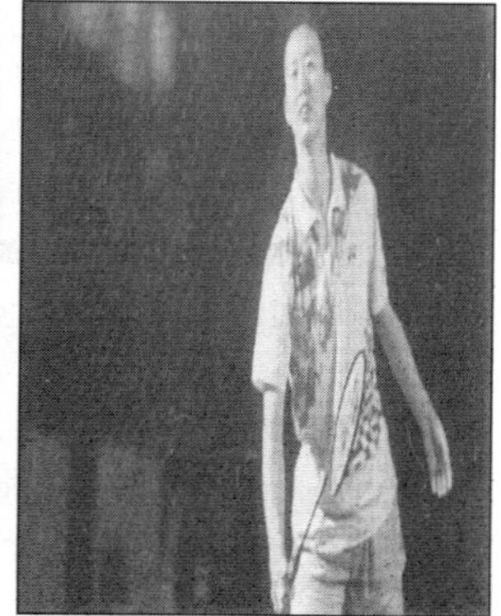

Figures 10.2.1, 10.2.2 and 10.2.3: The forehand cross-net drop

The Forehand Net Smash

The forehand net smash is a net play in which the player quickly and forcefully strikes the shuttle above the net so that it returns to the opponent with a sharp downward angle. It is the most offensive and threatening net shot. The key to a successful forehand net smash is opportunity. This means that the player needs to make a quick and correct judgment on the incoming stroke to determine if it is a good opportunity to use the net smash, and then react accordingly and promptly. An opportunity to use a forehand net smash is usually created after a powerful smash or a quick drop shot which leads to a weak return from the opponent (i.e., a net play that is too high above the net).

To execute the forehand net smash, the player holds the racket up in front of the body and above the head, and rotates the handle of the racket clockwise so that the "V" shape formed by the thumb and forefinger is on the left big facet of the handle. The wrist is extended slightly. During the downward motion, the player quickly snaps the wrist with a small, controlled forearm forward motion. Failure to control this forward motion may result in touching the net with the racket at the end of the play. (See Figure 10.3.)

Figure 10.3: The forehand net smash

The Backhand Net Plays

When the shuttle is on the backhand side, the player must turn his or her body and cross the right foot to the left front corner of the court in order to make a backhand net play. At the same time, the player switches to the backhand grip (i.e., the thumb is placed on either the left top small facet or the left big facet of the racket handle). The player holds the racket up and in front of the body at about eye level with the elbow bent slightly and the wrist abducted. The racket head is pointed at the approaching shuttle. This ready position is used to perform most of the backhand net plays.

The Backhand Net Drop

To perform the backhand net drop, the player first brings the racket back by slightly bending the elbow and abducting the wrist. After that, he or she adducts the wrist to carry the racket forward in a controlled manner and hit the shuttle softly. The racket face must be adjusted properly to ensure a good return.

Similar to the play made from the forehand side, there is also an advanced way to perform the backhand net drop shot. From the ready position, instead of bringing the racket backward, the player extends the elbow, rotates the forearm inward, and adducts the wrist to manifest a slicing motion from the left to the right so that the shuttle rolls over the net along its transverse axis. The point of contact is on the left side of the base of the shuttle. The ability of the player to control the force applied to the shuttle directly affects the quality of this net play. (See Figures 10.4.1, 10.4.2 and 10.4.3.)

Figures 10.4.1, 10.4.2 and 10.4.3: The advanced backhand net drop

The Backhand Cross-Net Drop

Another backhand net play is the backhand cross-net drop. From the ready position, for any backhand net play, the player suddenly drops the elbow down and rotates the forearm outward, followed by quick extension at the wrist. The player should grip the racket with his or her thumb on the top facet. (See Figures 10.5.1, 10.5.2 and 10.5.3.)

The Backhand Net Smash

To perform the backhand net smash, the player uses a special backhand grip (the thumb on the left big facet of the handle) and the strike stance (the right foot in front). The player holds the racket on the left side of the body and at about head height. The player then leaps forward, and while in the air, quickly and powerfully extends the forearm upward, forward and downward, and adducts the wrist. After hitting the shuttle, the player must bend the elbow immediately to withdraw the racket and avoid hitting the net.

Figures 10.5.1, 10.5.2 and 10.5.3: The backhand cross-net drop

Chapter 11

Badminton Strategies

Strategies in badminton are based upon:

1. the skill level, playing style, physical condition and psychological profile of the opponent, and
2. the player's own strengths.

In addition, strategy should help the player conceal his or her weaknesses in order to gain an upper hand over the opponent. There are specific strategies for singles and specific strategies for doubles.

Strategies for Singles

There are six major strategies that a player may adopt when playing badminton. They are:

1. attacking the back court,
2. serving for offense,
3. smashing and attacking the net,
4. attacking and controlling the four corners of the court.
5. using cross-court plays, and
6. turning defense into offense.

A beginner should attempt to master these six fundamental strategies to become a skillful player.

Attacking the Back Court

While utilizing this strategy, the player should repeatedly use both the overhead clear and the flat overhead clear to force the opponent to retreat to the back court area in a defensive mode. Once the return from the opponent is poor in quality (e.g., not high enough, not deep enough, etc.), the player can then use a variety of offensive shots to win the play. This strategy is especially effective when the opponent is weak in back court overhead offensive techniques and footwork.

Offensive Serving

If a player can effectively confine his or her opponent's offensive ability, he or she may control the outcome of the game. For this purpose, the player may use the short serve, the drive serve or the flat deep serve to start the play, because these types of serves force the opponent to choose defensive shots, such as the underhand clear, to return the play. This will create opportunities for the player to launch offensive attacks on the opponent's weaknesses. It is a good strategy to use if the opponent is weak on defense. Use of this strategy in the final, key moment of competition will usually cause an inexperienced opponent to panic and make mistakes.

For example, the offensive short serve leaves the opponent with only three choices of strokes; the underhand push shot, the underhand clear or the net play. If the opponent chooses to use the push shot or clear, and makes a poor return, the player can use various offensive strokes, such as a smash or drop shot, to gain the advantage. If the opponent plays a net shot, the player may quickly attack the opponent's weak spots with a push shot. To ensure this strategy's effectiveness, the player must know exactly where to deliver the serve.

Smashing and Attacking the Net

When the opponent returns the shuttle with an overhead clear, the player can combine the techniques of the smash and drop shot to force the opponent to make some poor returns. A smash or drop shot should be aimed at the areas near the sidelines. If the opponent returns a smash or drop shot to the front court near the net, the player can create more offensive opportunities by quickly charging the net and attacking the opponent with either the hairpin drop or the push shot.

Attacking and Controlling the Four Corners of the Court

This strategy requires a player to hit the shuttle accurately to the four corners of the court with a variety of strokes. Under this assault, the opponent has to move and change positions quickly in order to cover the court. Many times, the scrambled movement of the opponent results in either the failure to return to the center of the court after each shot and be ready for the next stroke, or the loss of his or her balance while moving around the court. This creates opportunities for the player to attack the opponent with offensive shots, such as the smash. This strategy is most effective when the opponent is slow, weak in flexibility and in poor physical condition.

Using Cross-Court Plays

Cross-court plays is a strategy in which the player attacks his or her opponent with the shuttle traveling across the court. If the opponent is slow and weak in flexibility, the cross-court play is a good strategy to use.

If the opponent starts the play with a forehand deep serve, the player may use a cross-court overhead clear to raid his or her forehand back court. When the opponent hits the shuttle straightway back to the deep backhand court, the player should strike back with a cross-court drop. If the opponent makes a net play to the forehand front court, the player can then make a cross-court net play. If the opponent returns the shuttle to the backhand front court, the player may quickly use a cross-court push shot to attack the opponent's deep backhand court, which forces the opponent to use a backhand stroke to respond to the attack. Because the opponent does not have enough time to prepare for the backhand return, the return will most likely be weak. The player may immediately seize this opportunity to launch his or her attack with a killing smash to win the rally. It is important to point out that while adopting this strategy into a player's game plan, it is not necessary to return every single shot with a cross-court stroke.

Turning Defense into Offense

When a player is on defense, it is important not to panic. As long as the player can react flexibly, return each stroke in a calm and intelligent way, and move the opponent with various shots, the player can still manipulate the opponent and keep the game under his or her control. The essence of this strategy is to wait for the best opportunity to win the rally. This may happen when the opponent makes an error in return (e.g., hits the shuttle under the net) or returns with a poor shot. For best results, the player should attempt to:

1. force the opponent to hit all the shots from the back boundary line,
2. return quickly to the center of the court and get ready for the opponent's assault, and
3. patiently wait for an offensive opportunity.

Strategies for Doubles

There are two important parts to doubles strategy—playing principles and positioning of players.

Playing Principles in Doubles

All playing strategies in doubles should be based on the following principles:

Principle 1

Doubles is a team game where partners must work together. The cooperation of the partners, who use good game strategies and court coverage, is essential to succeed in doubles.

Principle 2

Prior to the match, information about the opposing team, including its playing styles and commonly used strategies, must be obtained and reviewed. With this information, the team may then formulate an appropriate strategy.

Principle 3

The partners should feel confident with each other.

Principle 4

The players must make prudent observations. Through observation, the team may determine the strategic intention of the opponent and adjust its strategy accordingly.

Positioning of Players in Doubles

In general, players in doubles can position themselves in two formations: the side-by-side formation and the up-and-back formation. The rotational formation is deviated from these two formations.

The Side-by-Side Formation

In the side-by-side formation, each player covers half the court. This type of formation is advantageous in defense, but less effective in offense. The side-by-side playing formation is shown in Figure 11.1.

The Up-and-Back Formation

The up-and-back formation is good for offense. During an offensive play, one player stands close to the net to cover the front court, and the other covers the back court. The major problem with this type of formation is that it is less functional in defense because it leaves the sidelines open for attacks. The up-and-back formation is demonstrated in Figure 11.2.1 and 11.2.2.

Figure 11.1: The side-by-side playing formation

Figure 11.2.1 and Figure 11.2.2:
The up-and-back formation

The Rotational Formation

The rotational formation is a combination of the side-by-side formation and the up-and-back formation. The playing situation dictates the use of one formation or the other. If the team is on offense, it should quickly move into the up-and-back formation. If it is on defense, it should use the side-by-side formation.

Serving and Receiving in Doubles

The service court in doubles is shorter than that in singles. Therefore, a deep serve provides the opponent with an immediate opportunity to attack and put the team on defense immediately after the service. As a result, the short serve is used most frequently in doubles. If executed properly, the short serve forces the opponent to return the shuttle with a relatively favorable angle for the team to attack.

As the server prepares to serve from the right service court, the partner should take a position where he or she feels comfortable covering the other areas of the court. When the serve is made from the left service court, the partner does the same thing—positions himself or herself and returns shots in areas that the server is unable to cover after delivering the serve (see Figure 11.3).

Figure 11.3: Serving and receiving in doubles

When a team is receiving the serve, the receiver should stand very close to the service line because more than likely the serve will be short. The receiver should attempt to hit the shuttle at the highest point, as he or she possibly can, immediately after the shuttle passes the net. The higher the point of contact, the more opportunity the team will have to apply various offensive strokes. The partner should position himself or herself on the other half of the court and be prepared to assume either a defensive or offensive formation.

Doubles Strategies

Two-on-One Strategy

The playing strengths of the two players on a doubles team are usually not the same; one player is usually stronger than the other. Therefore, a good strategy is to repeatedly attack the weaker player. When a team is on defense, it should hit the shuttle to the weaker player, let him or her handle most of the shots, and patiently wait for offensive opportunities.

Turning Defense into Offense

In this strategy, the team patiently waits for opportunities to turn a defensive situation into an offensive one. Three methods can be used to do this:

Method 1: This method requires that the players use either the underhand clear or the push shot to hit the shuttle to the opponent's back court. When a team is on defense and the opposing team is attacking with smashes, it should use the underhand clear to return shots to the opponent's back boundary line area. If the opponent smashes again from the same side of the court, the player can hit the shuttle with a cross-court underhand clear to the opposing team's deep back court. If the smash is cross-court, the player should return it to the opponent straight ahead. If the opponent drops the shuttle to the front court, the player should use the same method to make the opponent move from side to side along the back boundary line. The opponent will eventually tire and relinquish its offensive position to the defending team.

Method 2: Similar to Method 1, the team uses either the underhand clear or the push shot to hit the shuttle to the opponent's back court. Once the opponent's smash is weak, slow and with a flat trajectory, the player can use a drive shot to bombard the opponent's back court. If the smash comes from the same side of the court, the player can hit a cross-court drive; if the shuttle arrives from cross-court, it can be returned straight ahead. The player must keep the racket high and be ready to hit another drive after returning a smash with a drive. Sooner or later the team will change its playing status from defensive to offensive.

Method 3: While repeatedly returning the opponent's offensive attacks (smashes and drop shots) with underhand clears, push shots and drives, every once in a while the players may try returning the shuttle to the opponent's front court. After doing that, the player needs to move immediately forward to cover the front court. So, the team turns its side-by-side formation into an up-and-back formation for offensive plays.

<u>Attacking the Middle Court</u>

When the opposing team uses the side-by-side formation on defense, the attacking team should aim its smashes between the two opposing players. This will cause confusion between the opposing players. They may either fight for the shot or hesitate to take the shot. Either way will lead to errors and create opportunities for the team to win the rally. This is a strategy often used when playing an opposing team that is weak in cooperation.

Attacking the middle court can also be utilized when the opponent uses the up-and-back formation. The team should hit the shuttle to an area near the sideline and between the opposing players. This may confuse the opposing players as they decide who will take the shot. This hesitation may result in a poor return and cost them the rally or a point. If the players on the opposing side lack cooperation and are inexperienced in handling mid-court plays, this strategy is strongly recommended.

<u>Attacking the Back Court</u>

If a team feels that the opposing team is weak on offense, it should utilize the overhead attacking clear and the push shot to force the opponent into staying on the back court. Even when returning a smash, the team can continue to attack the back court by hitting the shuttle deep and high. By doing so, the opponents have no choice but to maneuver from side to side around the back boundary line area. Once the opposing team makes a poor return, the team may initiate an offensive attack.

Blocking the Net While Attacking from the Back Court

When a team is on offense, the player covering the back court should smash as many of the returns from the opponent as possible. The player covering the front court should attempt to block as many shots as possible.

Chapter 12

Conditioning and Drills

Conditioning

Like any other sport, badminton players must be in good health and physical condition to play at an enjoyable and exciting level. Badminton is a great way to increase physical fitness and psychological wellness. The following methods may be used to help players prepare themselves for badminton practices and games, as well as improve their playing skills with solid psychological and physical conditioning.

Warmup and Flexibility

The following are some key points to remember before any warmup exercise.

1. Stretch all major muscle groups.
2. Do not bounce or use jerky movements.
3. Perform a gradual and easy stretch.
4. Hold a stretch for 10 to 20 seconds.
5. Slowly increase the stretch, as it feels more comfortable.
6. Do not hold a painful stretch.

Neck Mobility

1. Move the neck to each side touching ear to shoulder.
2. Turn the head from side to side.
3. Look down touching the chin to the chest.
4. Look up lifting the chin toward the ceiling.

Elbow and Wrist Stretch

Keeping the elbows straight, stretch one wrist into full flexion, palm up, by pressing upward with the other hand. Repeat on the other hand.

Arm Circles

Move the arms in large circles forward, then backward.

Overhead Shoulder Stretch

With hands joined overhead, reach toward the ceiling.

Pectoral Stretch against a Wall

With one arm at shoulder level against a wall, press the hand against the wall while turning the body away from the wall. Repeat with the other arm.

Triceps Stretch

Bend one arm above the head with the palm of the hand flat on the back. Then with the other hand gently stretch the triceps by pulling the elbow back. Repeat on the other arm.

Trunk Side Bend

While holding a racket by the handle and throat, bend the trunk as far as possible to both sides.

Anterior Thigh Stretch

With the left hand holding onto a chair for balance, lift the right foot and hold it with the right hand. Gently pull the foot toward the buttocks. Change sides and repeat.

Groin Stretch

Turning the right leg out, apply body weight to the right side and stretch the inner part of the left thigh. Repeat on the other leg.

Sitting Groin Stretch

Sitting on the floor, put the soles of the feet together and grasp the feet with both hands. Placing the elbows inside the knees, lean the upper body forward and gently press the knees outward.

Outside Thigh Stretch

Sitting on the floor with the left leg straight, bend the right knee and cross the right leg over the left so that the right foot rests outside the left knee. Place the left elbow on the outside of the right thigh and the right hand flat on the floor behind the body. Rotate the body to look at the right hand and at the same time pull the right knee with the left hand. Repeat on the other side.

Calf Stretch

With both hands against a wall and weight on the legs, keep the heels on the floor and the knees straight while moving the hips toward the wall. Feel the stretch just below the knee.

Achilles Stretch

As in the calf stretch above, while keeping the heels flat on the floor, bend the knees one leg at a time. Feel the stretch in the lower calf and Achilles tendon.

Upper Hamstrings and Seat Stretch

Sitting on the floor, pull the leg up, toward the chest with both hands. Repeat on the other leg.

Hamstring Stretch

Sitting on the floor with the sole of the right foot against the left upper inner thigh, reach for the toes of the left foot with both hands while keeping the left knee straight. Repeat on the other leg.

Ankle and Shin Stretch

Sit back on the heels with the toes resting flat on the floor.

Ankle Stretch

While standing, rest the toes of the right foot on the floor. Rotate the heel. Repeat with the other foot.

Conditioning Training

Strength and endurance training such as weight training, distance running, and other aerobic and anaerobic exercises should be included in the overall training plan. In addition to these general training methods, players need to develop the muscle groups that are particularly important for badminton. Players who need to improve their arm strength for badminton may use the following exercises:

Tennis Racket Swing

The player grips the tennis racket handle, as he or she would grip the badminton racket; then swings the tennis racket in front of the body using the same motions needed for badminton.

Tennis Racket Wall Drill

In this drill the player uses a tennis racket to hit the shuttle

Figure 12.1: Tennis racket wall drill

against a wall. This forces the player to use more arm strength and racket handling skill than just swinging the tennis racket. The extra weight of a tennis racket can significantly improve the player's arm strength and the accuracy of the wrist motion when hitting the shuttle with a tennis racket at the same speed as with a badminton racket. However, because a tennis racket is heavier than a badminton racket and the impact on the wrist and arm is far greater than the impact of a badminton racket, this drill should be performed with care. (See Figure 12.1.)

Practice Drills

Practice is essential to learn and improve badminton skills. Practice results in better skills. However, if the player does not choose appropriate practice drills, the quality of the practice can be questionable. Inadequate practices may even result in incorrect badminton techniques. The following suggestions will help instructors and students select appropriate drills for badminton practices.

Have Definite Purposes

Each practice needs to have specific objectives. The aim of any practice is to either learn new techniques or improve learned skills. Once a specific skill is identified, select drills which will help improve that skill.

Fit the Skill Level of the Player

Drills must be appropriate to the skill level of the player. Drills can maximize the results of the practice and prevent unnecessary injuries from happening. For example, the player who chooses to use a tennis racket for a wall rally drill must have sufficient arm and wrist strength. If not, the player is vulnerable to wrist or arm injuries.

Develop Mental Capacity

As previously discussed in Chapter 1 and Chapter 2, badminton is the fastest racket sport in the world and demands tremendous mental capacity to play it well. The mental development of the player is as important as the physical development. The drills selected should incorporate a high level of concentration on the practiced techniques and develop the player's mental capacity for the game.

Drills used in badminton practice may not be the same for everyone. As long as the basic principles are followed, the player or instructor should be flexible in choosing practice drills and creative in planning a workout. The following are the general categories of drills suggested for practice. These drills may be modified depending on the fitness level of the player. The drills can be practiced either alone or with a partner.

Drills for Fundamental Skills

<u>Racket Handling</u>

1. Learn the correct grip of the racket handle and swing the racket without hitting a shuttle.
2. Bounce a shuttle on the racket from low to high.
3. Scoop the shuttle from the floor.

<u>Ready Position and Footwork</u>

1. Place yourself in the ready position in the center of the court and in the receiving ready position in the service court. Feel your position on the court and know where the lines are around you.
2. Repeat each pattern of footwork from the ready position.
3. Combine different patterns of footwork and return to the ready position in the center of the court.
4. Run the footwork patterns on command to different areas of the court and return to the ready position whenever possible.

5. Move across the court or up and back on command.

Wall Drills

1. Use a wall to hit the shuttle with the underhand clear.
2. Use a wall to hit the shuttle with the drive.

Drills for the Service

1. Mark the targeted areas with tape and practice the deep, short, and drive serves to these areas.
2. Serve the deep serve by having your partner stand in the normal receiving position with the racket held overhead.
3. Tie a string 6 to 8 inches above the net and practice the short serve. The shuttle should travel over the net and under the string.
4. Practice both the forehand and backhand serves and find the most comfortable and adequate serving techniques for yourself.

Drills for the Underhand Clear

1. Stand in the area between the middle and two-thirds of the court from the net. Practice the forehand underhand clear by hitting a shuttle which is hit to you by a partner. Make sure the shuttle's trajectory is high and deep toward the opposing back boundary line.
2. Stand in the same area as above. Have your instructor or partner hit shuttles from the other side of the net to practice the forehand underhand clear. Return to the ready position after each stroke.
3. Have your instructor or partner smash the shuttles from across the net to practice both the forehand and backhand underhand clears. Return to the ready position whenever possible.

Drills for the Net Play

1. Stand relatively still between the net and the short service line. Have your partner drop shuttles to you from the other side of the net and return them with the hairpin drop.
2. Stand near the short service and the center line. Have your partner drop shuttles close to the net and return the shuttles barely clearing the top of the net. Return to the center spot after each stroke.

3. Take the same stance as above. Have your partner drop shuttles to your forehand side and practice the cross-court drop. Return to the center spot after each stroke.
4. Take the same stance as above. Have your partner drop shuttles to your backhand side and practice the cross-court drop. Return to the center spot after each stroke.
5. Have your partner hit shuttles just barely over the top of the net to different spots. Alternate between the forehand and the backhand strokes to practice different net plays.
6. With two or more players on the opposing side of the court, play a net drop game.

Drills for the Drive or Push Shots

1. With a partner on the opposing court, stand in the middle of the court and practice a rapid exchange of rally of both forehand and backhand drives. Increase the difficulty by either adding more power to the shots or moving closer to the net.
2. Have your partner serve drive serves and return the serves with the drive shot.
3. Have your partner hit low and fast drive shots to you. Return the shuttles with either forehand or backhand drive shots.
4. Have four players on one side of the court and two players on the other. The team of two players practices the drive shot with the team of four players.

Drills for the Smash and Drop Shots

1. Stand in the area between the middle and two-thirds of the court from the net. Have a partner hit short deep serves to you which you return with a smash.
2. Stand in the area between the middle and two-thirds of the court from the net. Have a partner hit short deep serves to you which you return with a smash or drop shot aimed at specific targeted areas.
3. Have two partners set up clears for you to practice the smash or drop shot whenever the shuttle is above your head and in front of you.
4. Have two partners set up clears for you. Alternate returns between the smash and drop shot.

Drills for the Round-the-Head Shot

1. Stand in the center of the court. Have your partner hit shuttles to you which you return with the round-the-head shot.
2. Have your partner hit shuttles to different spots on your non-dominant side. Return the shuttles with the round-the-head shot.

Modified Games for Singles

1. Play a singles game on the doubles court.
2. Play a singles game with a doubles team.
3. Play a singles game with a doubles team on the doubles court.
4. Start a singles game at a score of love-5 behind your opponent.
5. Start a singles game at a score of 5-10 behind your opponent.
6. Start a singles game at a score of 10-13 behind your opponent.
7. Play a singles game in which you cannot use the smash.

Modified Games for Doubles

1. Play a doubles game only in the side-by-side formation after the service.
2. Play a doubles game only in the up-and-back formation after the service.
3. Play a doubles game with an opposing team of four players.
4. Start a doubles game at a score of love-5 behind your opponent.
5. Start a doubles game at a score of 5-10 behind your opponent.
6. Start a doubles game at a score of 10-13 behind your opponent.

Appendix

Laws of Badminton*

As established by the International Badminton Federation
(*As of August 1998)

1. Court and Court Equipment

1.1 The court shall be a rectangle and lay out as in Diagram A. (Shown on the next page.)

1.2 The lines shall be easily distinguishable and preferably be colored white or yellow.

1.3 All lines form part of the area which they define.

1.4 The posts shall be 1.55 m (5'1") in height from the surface of the court. They shall remain vertical when the net is strained as provided in Law 1.10.

1.5 The posts shall be placed on the doubles side lines as in Diagram A (shown on the next page) irrespective of whether singles or doubles is being played.

1.6 The net shall be made of fine cord of dark color and even thickness with a mesh not less than 15 mm and not more than 20 mm.

1.7 The net shall be 760 mm in depth and at least 6.1 meters wide.

1.8 The top of the net shall be edged with a 75 mm white cloth tape doubled over a cord or cable running through the tape. This tape must rest upon the cord or cable.

1.9 The cord or cable shall be stretched firmly, flush with the top of the posts.

1.10 The top of the net from the surface of the court shall be 1.524 meters at the center of the court and 1.55 meters over the side lines for doubles.

1.11 There shall be no gaps between the ends of the net and the posts. If necessary, the full depth of the net should be tied at the ends.

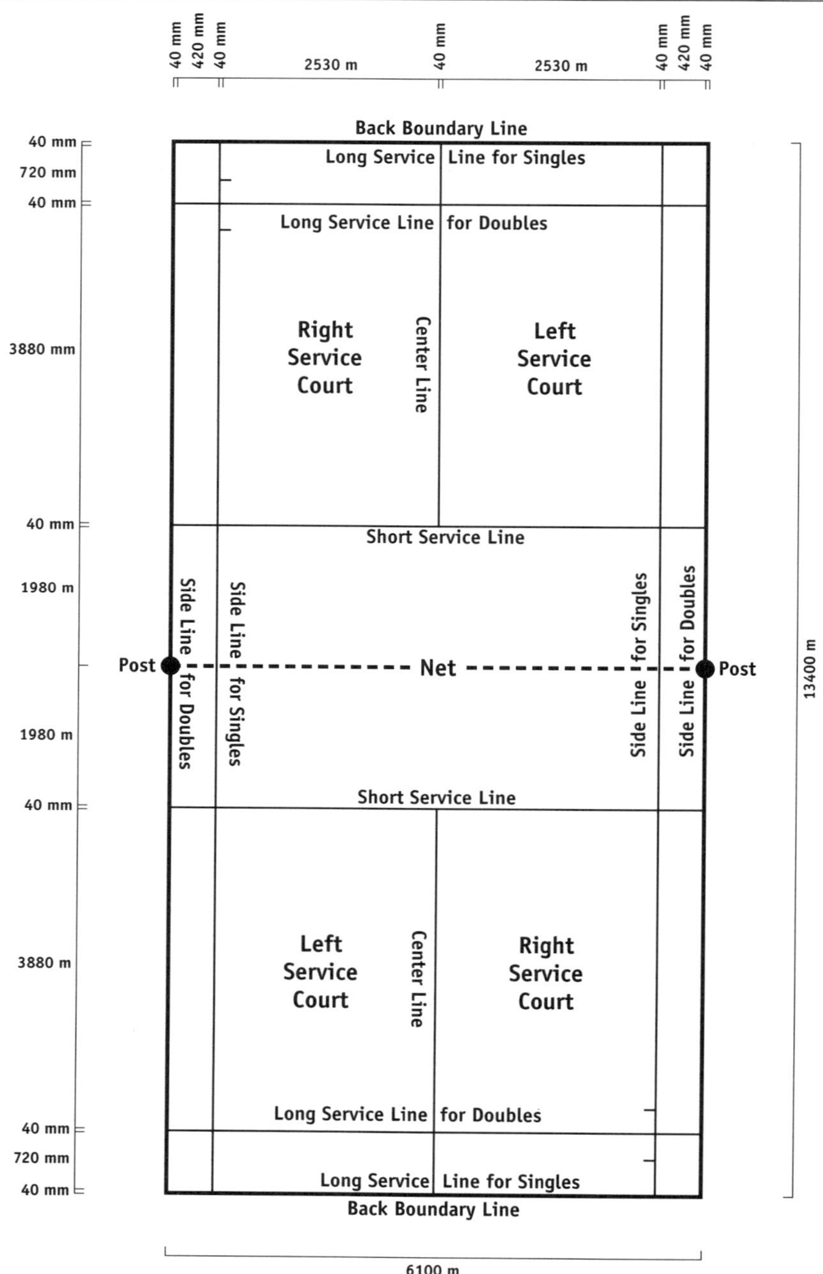

Note: Court which can be used for both singles and doubles play.

Diagonal length of full court: 14,723 m

Diagram A: The badminton court

2. Shuttle

2.1 The shuttle may be made from natural and/or synthetic materials. From whatever material the shuttle is made, the flight characteristics generally should be similar to those produced by a natural feathered shuttle with a cork base covered by a thin layer of leather.

2.2 The shuttle shall have 16 feathers fixed in the base.

2.3 The feathers shall be measured from the tip to the top of the base and in each shuttle shall be of the same length. This length can be between 62 mm to 70 mm.

2.4 The tips of the feathers shall lie on a circle with a diameter from 58 mm to 68 mm.

2.5 The feathers shall be fastened firmly with thread or other suitable material.

2.6 The base shall be: 25 mm to 28 mm in diameter and rounded on the bottom.

2.7 The shuttle shall weigh from 4.74 to 5.50 grams.

2.8 Non-feathered shuttle:

2.8.1 The skirt, or simulation of feathers in synthetic materials, replaces natural feathers.

2.8.2 The base is described in Law 2.6.

2.8.3 Measurements and weight shall be as in Laws 2.3, 2.4 and 2.7. However, because of the difference in the specific gravity and other properties of synthetic materials in comparison with feathers, a variation of up to 10 percent is acceptable.

2.9 Subject to there being no variation in the general design, speed and flight of the shuttle, modifications in the above specifications may be made with the approval of the Member Association concerned:

2.9.1 in places where atmospheric conditions due to either altitude or climate make the standard shuttle unsuitable; or

2.9.2 if special circumstances exist which make it otherwise necessary in the interests of the game.

3. Testing a Shuttle for Speed

3.1 To test a shuttle, use a full underhand stroke which makes contact with the shuttle over the back boundary line. The shuttle shall be hit at an upward angle and in a direction parallel to the side lines.

3.2 A shuttle of correct pace will land not less than 530 mm and not more than 990 mm short of the other back boundary line as in Diagram B.

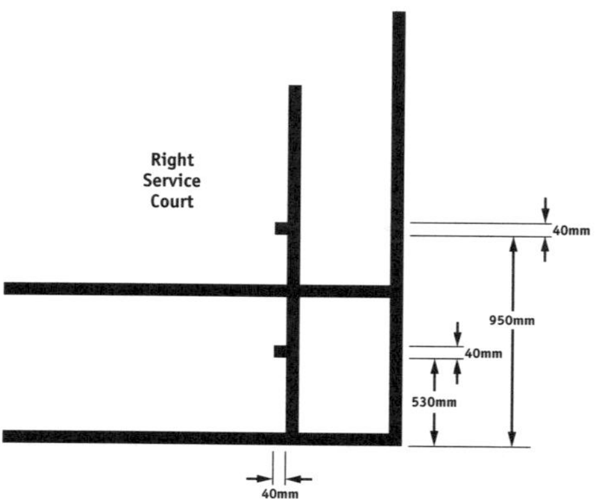

Optional Testing Marks for Doubles Court

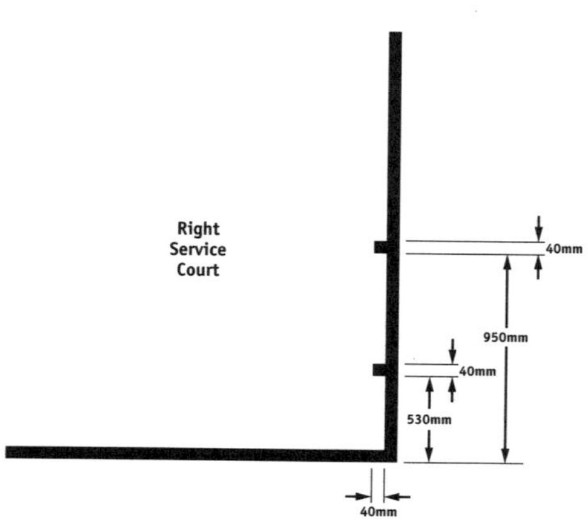

Optional Testing Marks for Singles Court

Diagram B: Testing a shuttle

4. Racket

4.1 The parts of a racket are described in Laws 4.1.1 to 4.1.7 and are illustrated in Diagram C.

4.1.1 The main racket parts are called the handle, the stringed area, the head, the shaft, the throat and the frame.

4.1.2 The handle is the part of the racket intended to be gripped by the player.

4.1.3 The stringed area is the part of the racket with which it is intended the player hits the shuttle.

4.1.4 The head bounds the stringed area.

4.1.5 The shaft connects the handle to the head (subject to Law 4.1.6)

4.1.6 The throat (if present) connects the shaft to the head.

4.1.7 The frame is the name given to the head, throat, shaft and handle taken together.

4.2 The frame of the racket shall not exceed 680 mm in overall length and 230 mm in overall width.

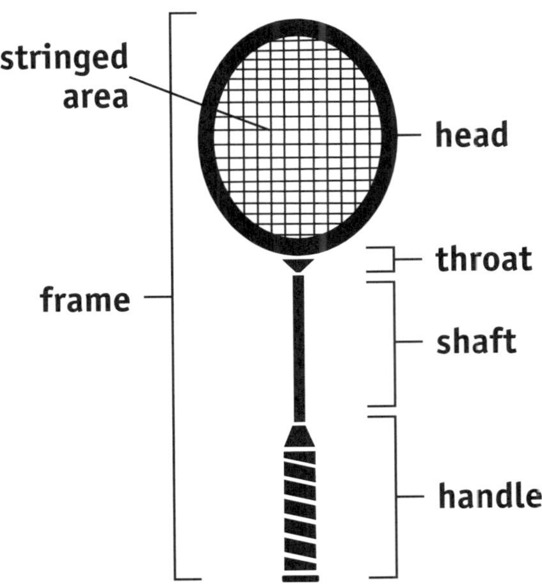

Diagram C: The racket

4.3 Stringed area:

4.3.1 The stringed area shall be flat and consist of a pattern of crossed strings either alternately interlaced or bounded where they cross. The stringing pattern shall be generally uniform and, in particular, not less dense in the center than in any other area.

4.3.2 The stringed area shall not exceed 280 mm in overall length and 220 mm in overall width. However, the strings may extend into an area which otherwise would be the throat, provided that the width of the extended stringed area does not exceed 35 mm and provided that the overall length of the stringed area does not then exceed 330 mm.

4.4 The racket:

4.4.1 shall be free of attached objects and protrusions, other than those used solely and specifically to limit or prevent wear and tear, or vibration, or to distribute weight, or to secure the handle by cord to the player's hand, and which are reasonable in size and placement for such purposes; and

4.4.2 shall be free of any device which makes it possible for a player to change materially the shape of the racket.

5. Equipment Compliance

The International Badminton Federation shall rule on any question of whether any racket, shuttle or equipment or any prototype used in the playing of badminton complies with the specifications. Such ruling may be undertaken on the Federation's initiative or upon application by any party with a bona fide interest therein, including any player, equipment manufacturer or National Organization or member thereof.

6. Toss

6.1 Before play commences, a toss shall be conducted and the side winning the toss shall exercise the choice in either Law 6.1.1 or Law 6.1.2.

6.1.1 to serve or receive first.

6.1.2 to start play at one end of the court or the other.

6.2 The side losing the toss shall then exercise the remaining choice.

7. Scoring System

7.1 A match shall consist of the best of three games, unless otherwise arranged.

7.2 In doubles and men's singles a game is won by the first side to score 15 points, except as provided in Law 7.4.

7.3 In ladies' singles a game is won by the first side to score 11 points, except as provided by Law 7.4.

7.4 If the score becomes 14-all (10-all in ladies' singles, the side which first scored 14 (10) shall exercise the choice in Law 7.4.1 or 7.4.2:

7.4.1 to continue the game to 15 (11) points, i.e. Not to "set" the game; or

7.4.2 to "set" the game to 17 (13) points.

7.5 The side winning a game serves first in the next game.

7.6 Only the serving side can add a point to its score (see Law 10.3 or 11.4).

8. Change of Ends

8.1 Players shall change ends:

8.1.1 at the end of the first game;

8.1.2 prior to the beginning of the third game (if any); and

8.1.3 in the third game, or in a match of one game, when the leading score reaches:

- 6 in a game of 11 points; or
- 8 in a game of 15 points.

8.2 If players omit to change ends as indicated by Law 8.1, they shall do as soon as the mistake is discovered and the shuttle is not in play. The existing score shall stand.

9. Service

9.1 In a correct service:

9.1.1 neither side shall cause undue delay to the delivery of the server and receiver have taken up their respective positions;

9.1.2 the server and receiver shall stand within diagonally opposite service courts without touching the boundary lines of these service courts;

9.1.3 some part of both feet of the server and receiver must remain in contact with the surface of the court in a stationary position from the start of the service (Law 9.4) until the service is delivered (Law 9.6);

9.1.4 the server's racket shall initially hit the base of the shuttle;

9.1.5 the whole shuttle shall be below the server's waist at the instant of being hit by the server's racket;

9.1.6 the shaft of the server's racket at the instant of hitting the shuttle shall be pointing in a downward direction to such an extent that the whole of the head of the racket is discernible below the whole of the server's hand holding the racket as in Diagram D;

9.1.7 the movement of the server's racket must continue forwards after the start of the service (Law 9.4) until the service is delivered; and

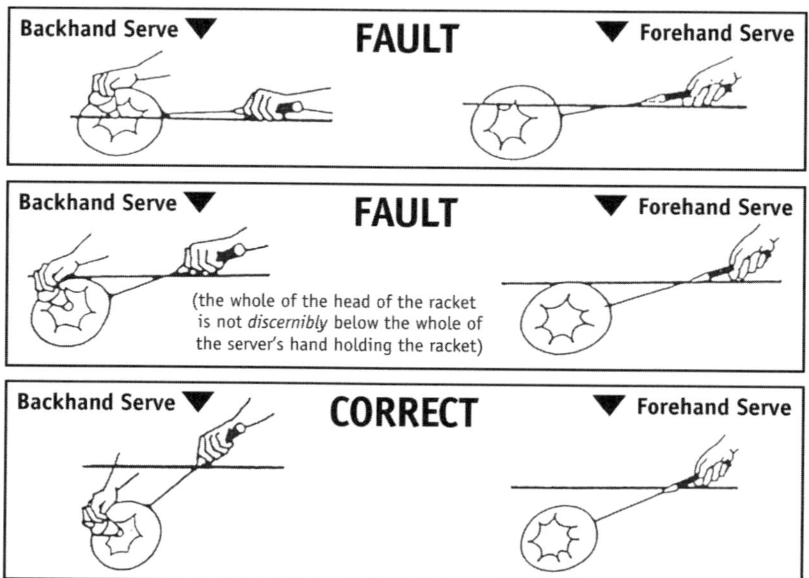

Diagram D: Hand position for serve

9.1.8 the flight of the shuttle shall be upwards from the server's racket to pass over the net so that, if not intercepted, it lands in the receiver's service court (i.e. on or within the boundary lines).

9.2 If a service is not correct by virtue of any of Law 9.1.1 to 9.1.8, it shall be a "fault" (Law 13) by the offending side.

9.3 It is a "fault" if the server, in attempting to serve, misses the shuttle.

9.4 Once the players have taken their positions, the first forward movement of the server's racket head is the start of the service.

9.5 The server shall not serve before the receiver is ready but the receiver shall be considered to have been ready if a return of service is attempted.

9.6 Once the service is started (Law 9.4), it is delivered when the shuttle is hit by the server's racket or, in attempting to serve, the server misses the shuttle.

9.7 In doubles, the partners may take up any positions which do not unsight the opposing server or receiver.

10. Singles

10.1 Serving and receiving courts:

10.1.1 The players shall serve from, and receive in, their respective right service courts when the server has not scored or has scored an even number of points in that game.

10.1.2 The players shall serve from, and receive in, their respective left service courts when the server has scored an odd number of points in that game.

10.2 The shuttle is hit alternately by the server and the receiver until a "fault" is made or the shuttle ceases to be in play.

10.3 Scoring and serving:

10.3.1 If the receiver makes a "fault" or the shuttle ceases to be in play because it touches the surface of the court inside the receiver's court, the server scores a point. The server then serves again from the alternate service court.

10.3.2 If the server makes a "fault" or the shuttle ceases to be in play because it touches the surface of the court inside the server's court, the server loses the right to continue serving and the receiver then becomes the server, with no point scored by either player.

11. Doubles

11.1 At the start of a game, and each time a side gains the right to serve, the service shall be delivered from the right service court.

11.2 Only the receiver shall return the service: should the shuttle touch or be hit by the receiver's partner, if shall be a "fault" and the serving side scores a point.

11.3 Order of play and position on court:

11.3.1 After the service is returned, the shuttle is hit by either player of the serving side and then by either player of the receiving side, and so on, until the shuttle ceases to be in play.

11.3.2 After the service is returned, a player may hit the shuttle from any position on that player's side of the net.

11.4 Scoring and serving:

11.4.1 If the receiving side makes a "fault" or the shuttle ceases to be in play because it touches the surface of the court inside the receiving side's court, the serving side scores a point and the server serves again.

11.4.2 If the serving side makes a "fault" or the shuttle ceases to be in play because it touches the surface of the court inside the serving side's court, the server loses the right to continue serving, with no point scored by either side.

11.5 Serving and receiving courts:

11.5.1 The player who serves at the start of any game shall serve from, or receive in, the right service court when that player's side has not scored or has scored an even number of points in that game.

11.5.2 The player who receives at the start of any game shall receive in, or serve from, the right service court when that player's side has not scored or has scored an even number of points in that game, and the left service court when that player's side has scored an odd number of points in that game.

11.5.3 The reverse pattern applies to the partners.

11.6 Service in any turn of serving shall be delivered from alternate service courts, except as provided in Laws 12 and 14.

11.7 In any game, the right to serve passes consecutively from the initial server to the initial receiver, and then that initial receiver's partner, then to the opponent who is due to serve from the right service court (Law 11.5), then to that player's partner, and so on.

11.8 No player shall serve out of turn, receive out of turn, or receive two consecutive services in the same game, except as provided in Laws 12 and 14.

11.9 Either player of the winning side may serve first in the next game, and either player of the losing side may receive.

12. Service Court Errors

12.1 A service court error has been made when a player:

12.1.1 has served out of turn;

12.1.2 has served from the wrong service court; or

12.1.3 standing in the wrong service court, was prepared to receive the service and it has been delivered.

12.2 If a service court error is discovered after the next service has been delivered, the error shall not be corrected.

12.3 If a service court error is discovered before the next service is delivered:

12.3.1 if both sides committed an error, it shall be a "let;"

12.3.2 if one side committed the error and won the rally, it is a "let;"

12.3.3 if one side committed the error and lost the rally, the error shall not be corrected.

12.4 If there is a "let" because of a service court error, the rally is replayed with the error corrected.

12.5 If a service court error is not to be corrected, play in that game shall proceed without changing the players' new service court (nor, when relevant, the new order of serving).

13. Faults

It is a "fault":

13.1 if a service is not correct (Law 9.1) or if Law 9.3 or 11.2 applies;

13.2 if in play, the shuttle:

13.2.1 lands outside the boundaries of the court (i.e. not on or within the boundary lines);

13.2.2 passes through or under the net;

13.2.3 fails to pass the net;

13.2.4 touches the ceiling or side walls;

13.2.5 touches the person or dress of a player; or

13.2.6 touches any other object or person outside the immediate surroundings of the court;

(Where necessary on account of the structure of the building, the local badminton authority may, subject to the right of veto of its Member Association, make by-laws dealing with cases in which a shuttle touches an obstruction.)

13.3 if, when in play, the initial point of contact with the shuttle is not on the striker's side of the net. (The striker may, however, follow the shuttle over the net with the racket in the course of a stroke);

13.4 if, when the shuttle is in play, a player:

13.4.1 touches the net or its supports with racket, person or dress;

13.4.2 invades an opponent's court over the net with racket or person except as permitted in Law 13.3;

13.4.3 invades an opponent's court under the net with racket or person such that an opponent is obstructed or distracted; or

13.4.4 obstructs an opponent, i.e. prevents an opponent from making a legal stroke where the shuttle is followed over the net;

13.5 if, in play, a player deliberately distracts an opponent by any action such as shouting or making gestures;

13.6 If, in play, the shuttle:

13.6.1 is caught and held on the racket and slung during the execution of a stroke;

13.6.2 is hit twice in succession by the same player with two strokes;

13.6.3 is hit by a player and the player's partner successively; or

13.6.4 touches a player's racket and continues towards the back of that player's court.

13.7 if a player is guilty of flagrant, repeated or persistent offenses under Law 16;

13.8 if, on service, the shuttle is caught on the net and remains suspended on top or, on service, after passing over the net is caught in the net.

14. Lets

14.1 "Let" is called by the umpire, or by a player (if there is no umpire), to halt play.

14.2 A "let" may be given for any unforeseen or accidental occurrence.

14.3 If a shuttle is caught on the net and remains suspended on top or, after passing over the net, is caught in the net, it shall be a "let" except on service.

14.4 If, during service, the receiver and server are both faulted at the same time, it shall be a "let."

14.5 If the server serves before the receiver is ready, it shall be a "let."

14.6 If, during play, the shuttle disintegrates and the base completely separates from the rest of the shuttle, it shall be a "let."

14.7 If a line judge is unsighted and the umpire is unable to make a decision, it shall be a "let."

14.8 A "let" may occur following a service court error; see Law 12.3.

14.9 When a "let" occurs, the play since the last service shall not count, and the player who served shall serve again, except where Law 12 is applicable.

15. Shuttle Not in Play

A shuttle is not in play when:

15.1 it strikes the net and remains attached there or suspended on top;

15.2 it strikes the net or post and starts to fall towards the surface of the court on the striker's side of the net;

15.3 it hits the surface of the court; or

15.4 a "fault" or "let" has occurred.

16. Continuous Play, Misconduct, Penalties

16.1 Play shall be continuous from the first service until the match is concluded, except as allowed in Laws 16.2 and 16.3.

16.2 Intervals not exceeding 90 seconds between the first and second games, and not exceeding 5 minutes between the second and third games are allowed in all matches in all of the following situations:

16.2.1 international competitive events;

16.2.2 IBF-sanctioned events; and

16.2.3 all other matches unless the Member Association has previously published a decision not to allow such intervals.

(In televised matches the Referee may decide before the match that intervals as in Law 16.2 are mandatory and of fixed duration).

16.3 Suspension of play:

16.3.1 When necessitated by circumstances not within the control of the players, the umpire may suspend play for such a period, as the umpire may consider necessary.

16.3.2 Under special circumstances the Referee may instruct the umpire to suspend play.

16.3.3 If play is suspended, the existing score shall stand and play shall be resumed from that point.

16.4 Under no circumstances shall play be delayed to enable a player to recover strength or wind.

16.5 Advice and leaving the court:

16.5.1 Except in the intervals provided in Laws 16.2 and 16.3, no player shall be permitted to receive advice during a match.

16.5.2 Except during the five minute interval described in Law 16.2, no player shall leave the court without the umpire's permission.

16.6 The Umpire shall be the sole judge of any delay of play.

16.7 A player shall not:

16.7.1 deliberately cause delay in, or suspension of, play;

16.7.2 deliberately modify or damage the shuttle in order to change its speed or its flight;

16.7.3 Behave in an offensive manner; or

16.7.4 be guilty of misconduct not otherwise covered by the Laws of Badminton.

16.8 The umpire shall administer any breach of Law 16.4, 16.5, or 16.7 by:

16.8.1 issuing a warning to the offending side;

16.8.2 faulting the offending side, if previously warned; or

16.8.3 in cases of flagrant offense or persistent offenses, faulting the offending side and reporting the offending side immediately to the Referee, who shall have the power to disqualify the offending side from the match.

17. Official and Appeals

17.1 The Referee is in overall charge of the tournament or event of which a match forms part.

17.2 The umpire, where appointed, is in charge of the match, the court and its immediate surrounds. The Umpire shall report to the Referee.

17.3 The service judge shall call service faults made by the server should they occur (Law 9).

17.4 A line judge shall indicate whether a shuttle is "in" or "out" on the line(s) assigned.

17.5 An official's decision is final on all points of fact for which that official is responsible.

17.6 An umpire shall:

17.6.1 uphold and enforce the Laws of Badminton and, especially call a "fault" or "let" should either occur;

17.6.2 give a decision on any appeal regarding a point of dispute, if made before the next service is delivered;

17.6.3 ensure players and spectators are kept informed of the progress of the match;

17.6.4 appoint or remove line judges or a service judge in consultation with the Referee;

17.6.5 where another court official is not appointed, arrange for that official's duties to be carried out;

17.6.6 where an appointed official is unsighted, carry out the official's duties or play a "let;"

17.6.7 record and report to the Referee all matters in relation to Law 16; and

17.6.8 take to the Referee all unsatisfied appeals on questions of law only. (Such appeals must be made before the next service is delivered or, if at the end of a game, before the side that appeals has left the court.)

Glossary

Alley: The six inch extended area on both sides of the court for doubles play.

Back alley: The area between the back boundary line and the deep service line for doubles.

Backcourt: The rear half of the court farthest from the net, in the area of the back boundary lines.

Backhand: The strokes performed on the non-dominant side of the body and with the racket across the body.

Back swing: Preparatory part of a stroke in which the racket is brought backward and leads to the forward swing to strike the shuttle.

Baseline: Synonymous term for back boundary line.

Bird: Another word for shuttlecock or shuttle.

Block: Holding the racket to rebound the shuttle into the opponent's side of the court without actively hitting the shuttle.

Carry: An illegal tactic in which the shuttle is held momentarily on the racket during the execution of a stroke.

Center line: Line that separates the left and right service courts.

Clear: A shot that hits the shuttle to the far end of the opponent's backcourt with a high trajectory.

Defense: A state of being under the opponent's attack; or a playing strategy that uses a significant portion of strokes with deep clears and slow drops.

Double hit: An illegal play in which the shuttle is hit twice or more times in a continuous stroke.

Drive: A shot with a fast and low, flat flight over the net.

Drive serve: A surprising and quick serve with a flat trajectory.

Drop: A shot hit softly that barely clears the net and falls on the front area of the opponent's court.

Fault: A violation of the playing rules in a game.

First serve: In doubles, the player who serves first in the right service court after each changeover of the service.

Foot fault: A violation of rules in which either the server or the receiver is not in a correct position during the serve.

Forecourt: The front area of the court between the net and the short service line.

Forehand: A stroke that is executed on the dominant side of the body.

Game: A unit of scoring points for victory: 15 points in men's singles and all doubles, and 11 points in ladies' singles.

IBF: International Badminton Federation, the international governing body in badminton.

Inning: The time during which a player or team holds the service.

"In" side: The side that holds the serve.

Let: A legitimate stop in play to allow a rally to be replayed.

Love: Term used for "zero" or nothing. "Love-all" (0:0) is called by the umpire to start a game.

Match: A series of games, usually two out of three, to determine a winner.

Net shot: A shot made from the forecourt that barely clears the net.

"Out" side: The side receiving the serve.

Overhead: Strokes in which the shuttle is hit above the head.

Racket: The implement used to strike the shuttlecock.

Rally: A continuous exchange of shots between opponents.

Ready position: A body stance from which the player may make a quick movement in any direction.

Receiver: The player who receives the serve.

Serve or service: The stroke placing the shuttle into play.

Service court: Designated area where the serve must be delivered.

Set: Method of extending a game to play off ties. The player reaching the tied score first has the option of setting.

Short service line: The line 6 ½ feet from the net which serves must reach to be legal.

Shuttlecock: Official term for the shuttle or bird; the projectile that is hit by the racket.

Side-by-side: A doubles formation in which the partners stand next to each other.

Smash: A hard overhead stroke that forces the shuttle sharply downward.

Supination: The outward movement of the wrist and arm used in all powerful backhand strokes.

USAB: USA Badminton. The national governing body for badminton in the United States, formerly known as, American Badminton Association and United States Badminton Association.

Underhand: A stroke that contacts the shuttle below the waist level.

Up-and-back: A doubles formation in which one partner plays in the front court and the other in the back court.

Badminton Test

Some of the ways to review badminton include:

History of Badminton

1. The origin and evolution of badminton.
2. The international and national governing bodies for badminton.
3. Current development of badminton around the world and in the Olympic Games.
4. Major international (IBF) tournaments.

Benefits of Playing Badminton

1. Physical demands for playing badminton.
2. Physical responses of the body while playing badminton.
3. Psychological responses of the mind while playing badminton.

The Court and Equipment

1. Dimensions and markings of the court.
2. Parts of a racket.
3. Court areas and lines for singles and doubles play.
4. Net and posts.

Badminton Terminology

1. Terms used to describe badminton techniques.
2. Terms used to describe playing strategies.
3. Terms used for practice drills and conditioning exercises.
4. Terms used for officiating.

Fundamentals in Badminton

1. Gripping the racket and handling the shuttle.
2. Positioning on the court.
3. Fundamental footwork for various strokes.

Basic Rules of Play

1. Etiquette for playing badminton.
2. Service rotation and reception.
3. Scoring system for singles and doubles.

Badminton Strategies

1. Strategies in singles.
2. Strategies in doubles.

Officiating Badminton Games

1. Serving and receiving faults.
2. Shuttle in play and not in play.
3. Suspension of play.
4. Misconduct and penalties.
5. Officials and appeals.

Badminton Test

True or False Questions

1. A rally is a series of consecutive returns of the shuttle across the net between players.
2. In ladies' singles, a game consists of 13 points.
3. A toss takes place in between the first and second games of a match.
4. "Carrying" means a momentary holding of the shuttle on the racket during the execution of a stroke.
5. It is legal for the racket to swing over the net in a follow-through motion as long as the shuttle was hit on the striker's side of the net and the opponent is not distracted.
6. A server may repeat the serve if he or she failed to hit the shuttle.
7. If the shuttle lands on the line(s), it is considered "out."
8. The height of the net at the center is 5′1."
9. Badminton is considered the fastest racket sport in the world.
10. The long, deep serve should target the receiver's back boundary line.

11. The player should always step with the dominant foot toward the shuttle to assume a strike step while executing either a forehand or a backhand underhand stroke.

12. At least part of both feet of the server and receiver must remain in contact with the surface of the court in a stationary position until the serve is delivered.

13. The drive serve should target the area that is near the receiver's short service line.

14. The short serve should target the area that is near the receiver's center line.

15. The short serve is used more frequently in singles than in doubles.

16. To execute a drop shot, the shuttle should be hit on the same spot on the racket as where a smash is hit.

17. When hitting a forehand overhead clear, the shuttle should be contacted well in front of the head.

18. The drive serve is designed to catch the receiver by surprise.

19. The most commonly used service in doubles is the short serve.

20. In doubles, both the server and the receiver must stand on their respective serving and receiving courts; but the partners of the two may position themselves anywhere on the court.

21. The first server in doubles may begin the service from either the right or left service court, depending on the score.

22. In doubles, it is considered a legal play if the partner of the receiver returns the serve.

23. Both the server and the receiver can step on any lines when the server is serving.

24. When a serve touches the net as it crosses, it is a "let."

25. The game is "in play" from the moment that the server begins to swing the racket to the instant that the shuttle touches the court floor.

26. Badminton was called "Poona" in China.

27. It is not a fault if the player steps under the net as long as the opponent is not distracted.

28. Players in doubles are required to hit in an orderly sequence during a rally.

29. Playing badminton can significantly contribute to the cardiovascular fitness of the players.

30. The name "badminton" comes from an ancient village in India.

31. The player should grip the handle of a racket very tightly.

32. The "frying pan grip" is used mainly in doubles.

33. The receiver should stand near the center line while receiving a serve in either side of the service courts.

34. The base position is an area about two steps behind the short service line and on the center line.

35. When executing a smash, the shuttle should be hit in front of the body with the head of the racket in front of the hand.

36. The forehand drive is a shot in which the shuttle is hit at an upward angle toward the opponent's back court.

37. The round-the-head shot should be used more often if the player has a weak backhand.

38. When receiving the serve in doubles, the receiver takes a stance closer to the net than in singles.

39. Side-by-side is a weak formation in doubles.

40. Basic doubles strategy calls for the weaker player to play up whenever possible.

41. If a men's single game is "set," a score of 15:14 ends the game.

42. In singles, the server serves from the left service court when the score is an even number.

43. A legal serve requires that the entire head of the racket be below the waist and the entire gripping hand be above the racket head while the shuttle is hit.

44. A smash played from the back court has less downward angle than one hit near the net.

45. The round-the-head shot is a forehand stroke played above the non-dominant side of the shoulder.

46. Underhand strokes are considered offensive shots.

47. Angle of return in badminton is relatively unimportant since the court is only twenty feet wide.

48. Crosscourt shots are best used when the opponent has not been drawn from the center position.

49. In singles, the object is to move the opponent forward and back using low serves, drives and drop shots.

50. In doubles, teams should decide to play side-by-side or up-and-back without changing this formation during a point of play.

51. Offense and defense are determined by the angle of the flight of the shuttle.

52. The side-by-side formation lends itself best to attack.

53. In mixed doubles, the lady should not make an attempt to return smashes and fast drives.

54. The serving side wins the point when a "let" is called.

55. In doubles, a good strategy is to attack the weaker player of the opposing team.

56. The term "second server" means the team which did not serve first in the game.

57. When setting, the player (team) reaching the tied score first has the option of setting.

58. The heavier the shuttle, the faster it flies.

59. It is considered legal to change the speed of the shuttle by bending the feathers.

60. In the third game of a doubles match, teams change ends when one team scores eight points.

Multiple Choice Questions

61. The game of badminton was named after a place in:
    a. India
    b. England
    c. China
    d. Denmark

62. The shuttlecock is not called by one of the following names:
    a. Shuttle
    b. Birdie
    c. Bird
    d. Flyer

63. In men's singles and all doubles, a game consists of:
    a. 11 points
    b. 17 points
    c. 15 points
    d. 13 points

64. "Set" means:
    a. a clear at an upward angle.
    b. a way to extend a tied game.
    c. carrying.
    d. the right to choose sides.

65. The smash is hit identically to the drop shot except:
    a. the shot is hit with more force.
    b. the contact point should be more in front of the head.
    c. the wrist is bent forward the same amount as when executing the drop shot.
    d. the follow though motion is larger.

66. Compared to the doubles service court, the singles service court is:
    a. shorter and wider.
    b. longer and wider.
    c. shorter and narrower.
    d. longer and narrower.

67. Compared to the singles playing court, in doubles, the playing court after the serve is:
    a. the same length but wider.
    b. the same length and width.
    c. the same width but longer.
    d. both longer and wider.

68. All of the following are important for the best execution of the overhead clear except:
    a. hitting off the back foot for power.
    b. rotating the trunk with a forward swinging motion.
    c. aiming for the short service line.
    d. having the point of contact above the dominant side of the shoulder.

69. In a men's singles game that is tied 14:14, the player who first reaches this score has the option to set the game to:
    a. 1 more point.
    b. 4 more points.
    c. 3 more points.
    d. 5 more points.

70. The net shots are best executed:
    a. near the back boundary line.
    b. the same as drop shots.
    c. when using backhand strokes.
    d. near the net area.

71. In singles, the short serve should be used:
    a. more often than the long deep serve.
    b. not at all.
    c. occasionally, as a surprise serve.
    d. only from the left service court.

72. The major disadvantage of up-and-back formation is that:
    a. it leaves the sidelines open for attack.
    b. it is hard to return when the shuttle goes between the players.
    c. the player in the "up" position will be attacked frequently.
    d. the player in the "up" position may use block shots.

73. In singles, the following strategies are commonly used except:
    a. keeping the opponent moving up and back.
    b. hitting a deep clear whenever you are in trouble.
    c. returning to the home base with a ready position after each shot.
    d. making low and short serves as often as possible.

74. Which of the following, in singles, is considered a poor strategy?
    a. Alternating drop shots and clears.
    b. Making cross court smashes to the opponent's forehand side.
    c. Driving the shuttle down the sidelines.
    d. Returning to the home base position after each shot.

75. Which of the following is the most frequently used way to initiate play in singles?
    a. The deep serve.
    b. The short serve.
    c. The flick serve.
    d. The drive serve.

76. The best target area for the long deep serve is:
    a. near the center of the service court.
    b. near the center line and the opponent's back boundary line.
    c. near the short service line and the center line.
    d. near the center line and side line.

77. All of the following are important for the best execution of the smash except:
    a. taking a position that is completely different from the forehand overhead clear.
    b. hitting the shuttle high and in front of the body.
    c. angling the shuttle on a downward trajectory.
    d. rotating the forearm and snapping the wrist rapidly and forcefully.

78. Which of the following is a stroke that is executed when the shuttle comes above the head?
    a. The backhand stroke.
    b. The forehand underhand stroke.
    c. The cross-net stroke.
    d. The overhead stroke.

79. The overhead strokes include the overhead clear, the smash, and:
    a. the forehand drive.
    b. the drop shot.
    c. the "hairpin" drop.
    d. the cross-net drop.

80. The forehand drive is a stroke that sends the shuttle:
    a. across the net with a sharp downward angle.
    b. horizontally across the net toward the back boundary line.
    c. across the net with an upward angle.
    d. just barely across the net and dropping near the net.

Completion

81. Shade the singles left service court in Court A provided below.
82. Shade the doubles right service court in Court B provided below.
83. Shade the singles playing court in Court C provided below.

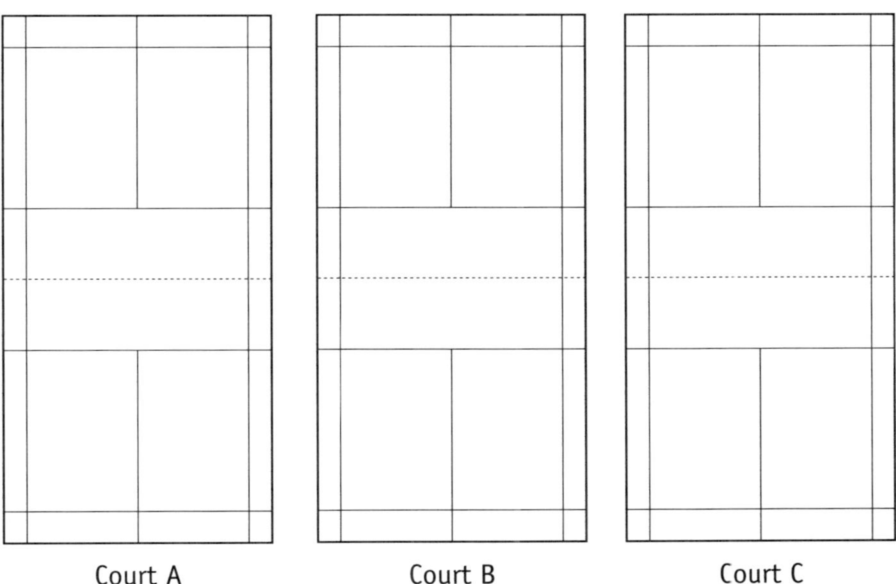

Court A Court B Court C

84. In doubles, what areas should be your targets when the opposing team plays the up-and-back formation? Mark the targeted areas in Court D provided below.

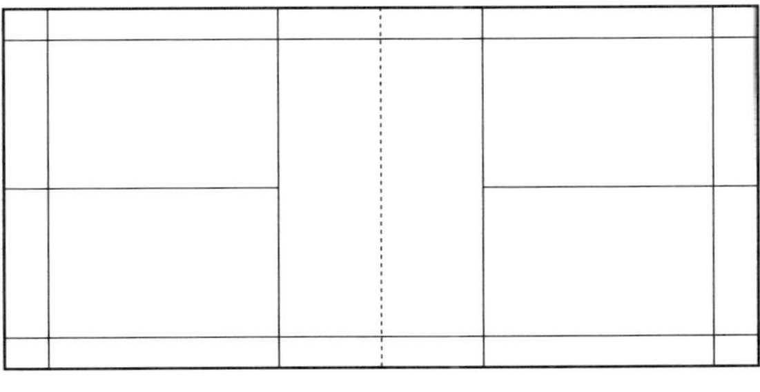

Court D

85. In doubles, what areas should be your targets when the opposing team plays the side-by-side formation? Mark the targeted areas in Court E provided below.

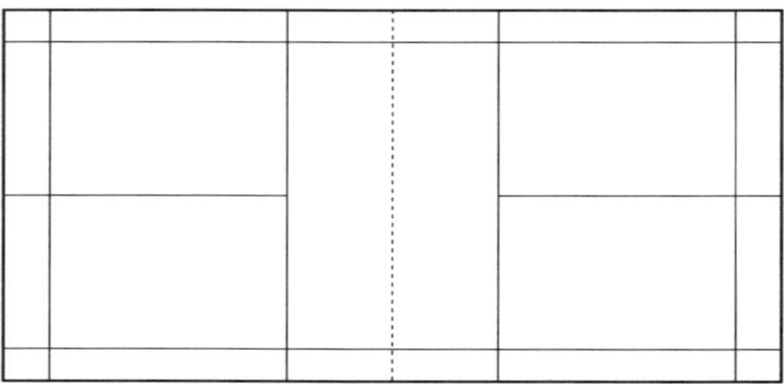

Court E

On Court F below, draw and number the flight patterns (in a direction from the left to right) for the following strokes:

86. The overhead drop shot.
87. The smash.
88. The short serve.
89. The drive shot.
90. The underhand clear.

Court F

Matching

Match the conditions below with the following answers.

A. Let B. Fault C. Set D. Shuttle not in play

_____ 91. The shuttle strikes the net or post and starts to fall towards the surface of the court on the striker's side of the net.

_____ 92. A line judge is unsighted and the umpire is unable to make a decision.

_____ 93. The shuttle touches the ceiling or side walls.

_____ 94. The shuttle passes through or under the net.

_____ 95. During service, the receiver and server are both faulted at the same time.

_____ 96. When a ladies doubles game is tied at 10:10.

_____ 97. The shuttle is hit twice in succession by the same player.

_____ 98. During the play, the shuttle disintegrates and the base completely separates from the rest of the shuttle.

_____ 99. In doubles, the shuttle touches a player's racket and then the player's partner.

_____ 100. The server serves before the receiver is ready.

Practice Test Answer Key

1. T
2. F
3. F
4. T
5. T
6. F
7. F
8. F
9. T
10. T
11. T
12. T
13. F
14. F
15. F
16. T
17. F
18. T
19. T
20. T
21. T
22. F
23. F
24. F
25. T
26. F
27. T
28. F
29. T
30. F
31. F
32. F
33. F
34. T
35. T
36. F
37. T
38. T
39. T
40. T
41. F
42. F
43. T
44. T
45. T
46. F
47. F
48. F
49. F
50. F
51. T
52. F
53. F
54. F
55. T
56. F
57. T
58. T
59. F
60. T
61. b
62. d
63. c
64. b
65. b
66. d
67. a
68. c
69. c
70. d
71. c
72. a
73. d
74. b
75. a
76. b
77. a
78. d
79. b
80. b
91. d
92. a
93. b
94. b
95. a
96. c
97. b
98. a
99. b
100. a

References

Bloss, M.V. and R.S. Hales. (1990, sixth edition). *Badminton*. Dubuque, Iowa: William C. Brown Publishers.

Canadian Badminton Association (1981). Skill Award Program: Teaching Manual. Vanier, Ontario, Canada: Sport Experts Inc.

Chafin, M.B. and M.M. Turner. (1988, second edition). *Badminton Everyone*. Winston-Salem, North Carolina: Hunter Textbooks Inc.

Cotten D.J., L.T. Paul and M. Li. (1995). *Badminton Basics*. Statesboro, Georgia: Press Express.

International Badminton Federation (1998). *International Badminton Federation Statutes*. Internet: http://www.intbadfed.org.

Peng, M. (1993). *Badminton*. Beijing, China: Beijing University of Physical Education.

USA Badminton (1997). *Badminton News*. 7(6).

Resources

International Badminton Federation (IBF)

The IBF is the governing body for international badminton competition throughout the world. It publishes the official Statutes with the laws of badminton as well as the interpretations of the laws. The IBF was founded in 1934 and originated from the Badminton Association of England. There were nine member countries when the IBF was founded. Today, its membership has risen to 138 countries and regions around the world.

The IBF's bimonthly official publication, *World Badminton*, contains reports on all major tournaments as well as articles of general interest about badminton. The IBF sponsors seven major international competitions which are listed as follows:

Thomas Cup - World Men's Team Championship

Uber Cup - World Ladies' Team Championship

World Championships - Individual Championship

Sudirman Cup - World Mixed Team Championship

World Juniors - World Individual Championship for Ages under 17

World Grand Prix Finals - Individual Competitions for the highest ranked players throughout a year

*World Cup - The World Cup series organized by the International Management Group (IMG) ended in 1997. The IBF is considering organizing a series of tournaments featuring the world's top players to replace the World Cup.

International Badminton Federation
Manor Park Place, Rutherford Way,
Cheltenham, Gloucestershire, GL51 9TU, UK
Tel: +44 1242 234 904
Fax: +44 1242 221 030
E-mail: info@intbadfed.org
Website: http://www.intbadfed.org

USA Badminton (USAB)

The USA Badminton is the official National Governing Body for the sport of badminton in the United States. It is based at the USA Olympic Center in Colorado Springs, Colorado. The USA Badminton was founded as the American Badminton Association in 1936, and the name United States Badminton Association (USBA) was adopted in 1978. The current name came into use after the 1996 Olympic Games. There are five geographic regions, fifty state associations and hundreds of member clubs under the USAB. The Board of Directors of the USAB is responsible for establishing policies for badminton in the United States. After the 1996 Olympic Games, the USAB established a national badminton team center in Colorado Springs. The USAB also established a nationwide badminton feeder program to identify elite and junior badminton athletes for the 2004 Olympic Games.

The USA Badminton publishes its official newsletter, *Badminton News*, eight times a year. The newsletter provides articles of interest to club and tournament players. It also gives national rankings, tournament schedules and tournament results. The USAB's official magazine is published biannually. All USAB members receive these publications. Additional subscriptions may be obtained through the national office.

USA Badminton
One Olympic Plaza
Colorado Springs, CO 80909
Tel: (719) 578-4808
Fax: (719) 578-4507
E-mail: USAB2004@rmi.net
Website: http://www.usabadminton.org

World Team Championships

Thomas Cup

Thomas Cup is the World Men's Team Championship. It was first staged in 1948 with the cup donated by the then President of the IBF, Sir George Thomas, Bart. The first competition was held in Preston, England. This also marked the beginning of Asian dominance in men's badminton. This phenomenon has continued to date. But, the recent successes by the Danes, particularly in singles, may signal a change for the future.

Originally the competition was held every three years but is now held every two years. The most recent Thomas Cup was held in Hong Kong in 1998. In 1984 the format of the Thomas Cup was changed to encourage more nations to participate.

Past Thomas Cup Winners

Contests	Competing Associations	Champion
1948-49	10	Malaya
1951-52	12	Malaya
1954-55	21	Malaya
1957-58	19	Indonesia
1960-61	19	Indonesia
1963-64	26	Indonesia
1966-67	23	Malaysia
1969-70	25	Indonesia
1972-73	23	Indonesia
1975-76	26	Indonesia
1978-79	21	Indonesia
1981-82	26	China
1984	34	Indonesia
1986	38	China
1988	35	China
1990	53	China
1992	54	Malaysia
1994	51	Indonesia
1996	56	Indonesia
1998	49	Indonesia

Uber Cup

Uber Cup is the Ladies' World Team Championship. It is an equivalent competition to Thomas Cup. Uber Cup was first proposed in 1950 by the former English Champion, Betty Uber. Due to financial reasons, it was not played until 1956-57. The championship was named after its donor. Uber Cup was not held at the same time as Thomas Cup until 1984. The format of Uber Cup is the same as Thomas Cup.

Japan used to be the strongest team in Uber Cup competition. Presently, it is a fight between Chinese and Indonesian teams for supremacy. The results of the past winners to date are as follows:

Past Uber Cup Winners

Contests	Competing Associations	Champions
1956-57	11	USA
1959-60	14	USA
1962-63	11	USA
1965-66	17	Japan
1968-69	19	Japan
1971-72	17	Japan
1974-75	14	Indonesia
1977-78	16	Japan
1980-81	15	Japan
1984	23	China
1986	34	China
1988	31	China
1990	42	China
1992	44	China
1994	44	Indonesia
1996	47	Indonesia
1998	40	China

IBF Approval Scheme

The International Badminton Federation currently approves the following equipment for international play:

Nets

Yonex
Victor

Net Posts

Erhard

Playing Surface

Mondosport
Nagase-Kenko
Taraflex
Victor Pro Court

Feather Shuttlecocks

Al Sheng	Tenlux AS101 Top
Babolat	Aeorflex Tour
Carlton	Dunlop Green
CFJ Trading	LS International Tournament
Chun-Yue Corp	SC Balance CSL 305
Crocodile Sdn Bhd	Crocodile Tournament
Double Fish Sports Goods Factory	Jinque AAA
Gadjah Mada	International Red
Gadjah Mada	Samurai
Gosen Co Ltd	Gosen Gold S-200
Indo-cock Badminton Shuttlecock Industry	Indo-cock Green
Intersport	Tecnopro TEC 400
Jago & Company	Snowpeak Superior C1101
Kao Ding Trading Co Ltd	Airshuttle Tournament
Loy Fok Hing	Tronex Tournament
Mizuno	Technoflite 400ED
Mizuno	Technoflite 500ED
Nimatsu	Tournament
P T Garuda Budiono Putra	Garuda International
Pingyang Huanyu Sports Goods	Break 101A
Postsky	Hi-Qua (blue)
RJ Badminton Europe	RJ Tournament 101
RSL	Tourney No.1
Saxon & All-England	Pro-Saxon Aerodynamic
Shanghai Badminton Factory	Aeroplane G1130
Shankyo Sports Co Ltd	Shankyo First Grade
Trump Sports	Trump T-101
Union Perfect	Prima International Grade
Victor	Champion
Wah Hing Creation	Joerex Tournament No.100
Xumax International	Xumax X1
Yonex	Tournament
Yueh Ma Sporting Goods	Kawasaki Top A
Zhejiang Ligh Industrial Products I/E Corp	Sealion Superior Tournament